for Jim Bruer

Toronto, July 1/01

Arian Wittedeen

*A Century of Greenkeeping*

# A Century
# of Greenkeeping

GORDON WITTEVEEN

Ann Arbor Press
Chelsea, Michigan

This book represents information obtained from authentic and highly regarded sources. Reprinted material is quoted with permission, and sources are indicated. A wide variety of references are listed. Every reasonable effort has been made to give reliable data and information, but the author and publisher cannot assume responsibility for the validity of all material or for the consequences of their use.

Neither this book nor any part may be reproduced or transmitted in any form or by any means, electronic or mechanical, including photocopying, microfilming, and recording, or by any information storage or retrieval system, without permission in writing from the publisher.

Ann Arbor Press
310 North Main Street
P.O. Box 20
Chelsea, MI  48118
www.sleepingbearpress.com
Ann Arbor Press is an imprint of Sleeping Bear Press

Printed and bound in the United States.
10 9 8 7 6 5 4 3 2 1

Library of Congress Cataloging-in-Publication Data

Witteveen, Gordon.
A century of greenkeeping / Gordon Witteveen.
p. cm.
ISBN: 1-57504-161-8
1. Golf courses—Maintenance—Canada—History.
2. Turf management—Canada—History. I. Title

GV 975.5 .W58 2001
796.352'06'9—dc21

2001022378

*This book is dedicated to the young men and women who follow in our footsteps.*

The Premier
of Ontario

Le Premier ministre
de l'Ontario

Legislative Building
Queen's Park
Toronto, Ontario
M7A 1A1

Hôtel du gouvernement
Queen's Park
Toronto (Ontario)
M7A 1A1

Ontario

Dear Friend:

When we tee-off on the first hole, we're usually not aware of all the work that's been done since yesterday's last foursome finished off.

The course superintendents and the greenkeeping crew were out late at night and back on the course early in the morning, getting the turf in playing condition.

When you think about all the divots, the ball marks and other damage that can be done to a golf course in one round, let alone a day or a whole season, it's amazing that our courses in Ontario are in such terrific shape. It's a real testament to the dedication of the course staff.

That's why I was so pleased to hear that Gordon Witteveen has taken the time to record the history of greenkeeping, on behalf of the Ontario Golf Superintendents Association.

Over the last 75 years, the game of golf has come a long way in our province. It's grown in popularity. The hard work of our superintendents helped make this great game accessible to more and more people.

Few pleasures in life are more enjoyable than playing on a well-kept golf course. This book is a great tribute to the hard working people who are responsible for those courses.

They have earned our most hearty thanks.

Sincerely,

Mike Harris
Premier of Ontario

# *Foreword*

In *A Century of Greenkeeping*,
Gordon Witteveen provides the
reader with an understanding of the
people and the organizations that
were largely responsible for the art
and science of greenkeeping as we
know it today. Often, using their
own words, he presents the views
and the ideas of these early innova-
tive practitioners, and he details
how they helped the profession
evolve.

*Clayton Switzer*

Changes in the profession were
related to the development of organizations such as the Ontario
Golf Superintendent's Association and the Canadian Golf Superintendent's Association, that facilitated the exchange of
ideas, recognized and supported education and research in
turfgrass management, and developed publications that
helped make up-to-date information available. This book rec-
ognizes and applauds the people behind these organizations
who "made it happen." It also gives us a better understanding
of the challenges they faced in the early days of the profession.

In recent years, golf courses have become oases of environmental friendliness amid our ever-increasing urban sprawl.
The author of this book, Gordon Witteveen, has been a leader

and role model and mentor for many of today's golf course superintendents who have fostered increased stewardship of resources and environmental sustainability. In addition, his many other contributions to the profession of greenkeeping throughout his career well qualify him to be the author of this book and indeed, to be included among the "giants of the profession."

*A Century of Greenkeeping* provides the background to the development of the profession, and it will continue to provide inspiration to future golf course superintendents to strive to become even more effective in turfgrass management and environmental responsibility.

CLAYTON SWITZER
June 2000

# Acknowledgments

The idea for this book came from Paul Dermott who managed to convince a committee chaired by Jim Wyllie that I should be the author. Since the beginning, Jim Wyllie, Paul Dermott, and the committee have been a source of support and encouragement.

Most of the research was done at two places: The museum at Golf House in Oakville and the GCSAA library in Lawrence, KS. Karen Hewson at Golf House and Susanne Clement in Lawrence were both very helpful. The early minutes of the Ontario Greenkeepers Association (1937–1957), a document uncovered by Jim Wyllie, proved invaluable. So did the back issues of *The Canadian Golfer* and *The Golf Course Reporter*. Early documents of the Western Ontario Greenkeepers Association, preserved by John Piccolo and made available by Rick Serrao, helped a great deal.

No book on the history of any aspect of golf could be written without reading the history of *Golf in Canada* by James Barclay. Jim answered my calls for help time and again and reviewed the first chapter in detail. We thank him for his contribution.

Many of the senior members of our group proved to have retentive memories. Their contributions were invaluable. Keith Nisbet, David Moote, Bob Moote, Dave Gourlay, and Art Dodson deserve special mention. Paul White and John Arends helped sort and identify numerous old photographs. Mark Schneider proved invaluable in checking details. Jim

Flett did much tedious work on the biographical section. Jeff Mingay, an aspiring golf writer from Windsor, put me in touch with Lyle Gray in Palm Springs, CA. The result was a whole chapter on John Gray who must have been one of the greatest greenkeepers of the twentieth century. We should all be proud of his contributions to the profession of greenkeeping.

The fact that the OGSA has an efficiently run office under the direction of Dorothy Hills made the writing of this book a whole lot easier. Bill Fach at York Downs reviewed my first book and he did so again with the second. There are sure to be some people that I have forgotten to thank. I do so now.

GORDON WITTEVEEN
Toronto
Summer, 2000

# Contents

▲
―――――――
▼

# CHAPTER I

# Golf in the Beginning

When golf came to Canada in the latter part of the nineteenth century, it was first played on large open spaces near the major centers of the country. In the case of Quebec City, golfers chose the Plains of Abraham, a battlefield where General Wolfe defeated Montcalm for the dominance of Lower Canada. In Montreal, golf was played at Fletcher's Field, a park on top of Mount Royal where golfers shared the course with ladies pushing prams. In the cities of Brantford and Halifax, the first golfers played on the common in the center of the cities which consisted of large expanses of grass available also to cricketers and, at times, even livestock. In Niagara-on-the-Lake, the early golfers played in the shadows of a century-old fort and across trenches and casements that had seen use in the War of 1812.

## The Early Courses

Except for Quebec City and Niagara-on-the-Lake, golfers soon tired of sharing their course with other people in the parks, on the battlefields, and on the commons and they moved to more suitable terrain where they could practice their sport in more subdued privacy. In the case of Quebec City, the golfers stayed on the Plains for almost 40 years and at Niagara-on-the-Lake, golf is still played on the very same field where it all began.

The first golfers were mostly transplanted Scotsmen who had played the game in their native land and brought along their sticks when they emigrated to Canada. Some early Canadian golfers were exposed to the game on their visits to Scotland. They in turn bought clubs and balls from Old Tom Morris at St. Andrews. Upon their return to Canada they joined the growing legion of golfers on Canada's early courses.

The first golf courses in Canada were often quite primitive and were laid out by the very same people who had imported the game. The early greens were flattened with shovels and rakes and rolled with wooden rollers. When sprigs of grass raised their heads, they were cut with a razor sharp scythe. Older men who had been trained to use the scythe knew how to cut new grass to perfection. The best time to use the scythe is early in the morning while the grass is wet with dew. The grass is more firm and the scythe will cut more easily and less physical effort is required to mow the grass. Of course the opposite is true in the case of the mechanical mower. To be able to use a scythe and to sharpen a scythe were skills that took a long time to acquire. Mowing by scythe was labor-intensive and and at first, only the wealthy could afford the luxury of a fine lawn.

After scything a green, it was necessary to remove the clippings by sweeping the turf with a birch broom or a biesum (as such implements were and are still known in Scotland). The birch broom also had an important other function: It helped break up the objectionable worm casts.

The first reel-type lawnmower was invented in England in 1823 and slowly became available to North Americans who demanded a perfect green sward that they had seen in English gardens. The establishment of golf courses increased the demands for push-type reel mowers in America and soon lawn mowers were mass-produced by American industry. From the beginning of golf on this continent, push-type reel mowers were available but catchers came later.

Since the early courses had been laid out largely on areas that were already covered with pasture grasses (mainly blue grasses, red top, and clover) the fairways developed naturally. There may have been other grasses and weeds in this mixture, but they would gradually disappear under a constant regimen of cutting the grass short with a single horse mower or with a flock of sheep.

The first recorded purchase of a 30-inch reel type mower took place at the Victoria GC on Vancouver Island in 1903. It was made by the Pennsylvania Lawn Mower Company and the quoted price was $100. The draw bars for the horse and the sulky seat were an extra $25. We may assume that golf clubs in Ontario made similar purchases. It is hard to imagine that a single reel-type mower was sufficient to cut all the fairways on a golf course. Of course it was not. We must remember that the fairways did not start until about one hundred yards from the tee and they were quite narrow strips.

The tees were small square mounds, mostly void of grass. When golf was in its infancy, there was no need for an elaborate teeing surface. In fact, at first, golfers were required to tee-off within a club length from where they had holed out. Golfers (or their caddies) fashioned a small mound of loose dirt on which they placed their gutta-percha ball and flailed away.

When Fred Hawkins, longtime greenkeeper at Toronto

Lakeview GC, came to Canada from England in 1906, he spent a day helping lay out a course. Hawkins describes his first experience on the golf course in Canada:

> *I would like to tell you of my first experience in seeing a golf course laid out. The club I am speaking of was a 9-hole course under the supervision of the professional, who had under him a head groundsman, as he was called in those days. This professional, who in later years was recognized as one of the leading golf architects, was about to lay out nine more holes and as he was trying to get me interested in golf, he invited me along.*
>
> *We started out with the groundsman carrying a bundle of stakes and a hammer until we came to a spot where they drove in four stakes 12 ft apart, which they called the 10th tee. After traveling further on, they drove in a stake, walked around it, then decided to take it a few yards further down into a hollow where they drove in four stakes 24 yards apart. This was the 10th green. I asked why they moved it from the first position and was told that the green would get more moisture down there. This was the procedure all around the course. The only difference being that they made one or two greens round instead of square.*
>
> *What bunkers were put in were across the fairway, pits of about one foot deep, eight feet wide and twenty-five feet long, with the soil thrown to the back about two feet high. Their methods of making greens was simply to cut and roll and topdress with some compost and a little bone meal and work them up out of the old sod that was there. In six weeks we were playing on them.*

Although the incident that Hawkins described occurred more than 30 years after golf became established in Canada, it can reasonably be surmised that the methodology had not changed significantly during that time period. If anything, it must have been even more primitive. At least the professional who laid out some of the early courses knew how to play the game. (Almost certainly this was golf professional George Cumming from the Toronto GC, who is considered to be the dean of golf professionals in Canada and who helped start the CPGA in 1911).

# From Groundsman to Greenkeeper

The centennial booklet of the Brantford GC mentions that the club hired a caretaker who "was paid 15 cents an hour to push a handmower over the greens and to keep the course in some sort of shape. He was helped by a herd of cattle which grazed on the course." The caddies meanwhile were paid 10 cents for nine holes. Strangely, the Brantford chronicle never again mentions the efforts of its successive greenkeepers in their 100-year history.

To the contrary, the Royal Montreal GC has been very generous in its praise of greenkeepers during its 100-year history. Once the Royal Montreal GC became established at Fletcher's Field in 1880, it hired a Mr. McNulty as a groundsman and paid him $20 "for his services in connection with caring for the Green." It must be explained that the "Green" is a very ancient term, meaning the whole course including the putting greens. The term "fair-greene" is an old term for fairway. So, although McNulty was charged to look after the green, it was felt that his efforts were insufficient and he did not become known as the greenkeeper. The following year, 1881, Royal Montreal hired William. F. Davis, a Scot who had been assistant professional at an English golf course, to be its golf professional and to do double service as greenkeeper, as was customary in that period of time. These were the instructions Davis received from the club captain at the time:

*If you take every afternoon a wheelbarrow and spade or the small lawnmower and take the green from hole to hole, removing all objectionable obstacles and cutting all the grass that can be cut, you would soon have the green in a very different state from what it is.*

There is no mention of a horse drawn mower for the fairways, but in any case Davis would have none of it and he either resigned on the spot or his services were terminated. We don't know which. He thereby became the first professional and the first greenkeeper in North America whose record of employment was also one of the shortest. He returned to Britain but came back to Canada and the Royal Montreal GC at a later date. This time he lasted for five years but was then lured to New York, where he gained everlasting fame for laying out the original holes of the Shinnecock GC.

In spite of this unfortunate experience Royal Montreal built a solid reputation in our industry of hanging onto their managerial staff. There have been only five professionals and six golf course superintendents in the 125-year history at the club. For many years thereafter, the club hired only Scottish greenkeepers. Sam Elliott, who served for many years, was the last greenkeeper recruited from Scotland. After Elliott, Royal Montreal hired Canadian golf course superintendents.

After the demise of Mr. Davis, the club hired Mr. Rogers as its greenkeeper at a salary of $8.00 per month for seven months. Mrs. Rogers was hired to look after the clubhouse and to make the fires. She was paid $6.00 per month. This

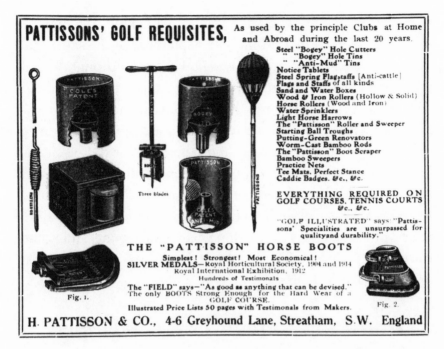

*Pattisson of England was the supplier of choice to the golf industry in the early days of golf.* The Canadian Golfer, *May 1916.*

energetic couple looked after the Montreal golfers both on and off the course and they served the members well.

The Victoria GC on Vancouver Island was established in 1893 on terrain that it occupies to this day. It began as a 9-hole course and was later expanded to 18 holes. Several of the original greens are still in place but most have been made over. The Victoria GC remains an historic monument to golf in our country.

In Halifax, golf was first played on the Studley grounds near the center of the city. The Halifax GC held its first meeting in 1896, where it was decided "to engage a caretaker for $6.00 per week." Halifax GC later became the Ashburn GC.

With both greenkeeping and golf in their infancy, it is not surprising that the great English golfer, Harry Vardon, found our courses lacking when he came to play exhibition matches in North America in 1900. In late September of the same year, Vardon played a match at Rosedale GC and although "a half dozen men and a team of horses had been out rolling and cutting the course by lantern the previous night," Vardon was not impressed. In no gentle terms he criticized the roughness of the course and the lack of sand bunkers. Nor did he change his opinions of Canadian courses when he played more exhibitions in Montreal and Vancouver. Vardon's comments forced Canadian clubs to take another look at the maintenance of the courses. Something had to be done and something was done. The clubs turned to their Scottish professionals for help.

## Golf Professionals as Greenkeepers

The first greenkeepers were also the golf professionals, not only in Scotland and England but also in Canada and the United States. According to Horace Hutchinson, the British golfer and writer, the hierarchy of the golfing profession in the latter part of the 1800s was as follows:

> *The green-keeper, engaged by the club at a certain annual salary to look after the ground, arrange the tees, and read the Riot Act to small boys who play off the green with their irons, and generally to act as custodian. He will be the keeper of a club makers' shop, in which he will probably do a certain amount of work at spare moments, and will usually have several man in his employ. He will also be the overseer of one or more horny-handed sons of toil who, under his directions, roll, sweep and mow the greens and fill up iron-skelps and other wounds in the ground, at discretion. Besides this, he will be open to engagements to play a round of the links when required, at*

*a fixed fee, whether with skilled players or with tiros who need instruction.*

Hutchinson goes on to list some of the requirements for greenkeepers:

*He will need to have some knowledge of turf-cutting, and the technical knowledge generally necessary for keeping the turf on the putting greens in fine order. He will need to be an observer of the growth of grasses. If he sees an iron cut, he at once has it filled up level with sand, which experiment has convinced him encourages a growth of young grass.*

Hutchinson's idol is Old Tom Morris at St. Andrews whom he calls "The High Priest of Professional Golf," recognizing that Old Tom is also the custodian of the Green.

The high priest in Canadian professional golf was George Cumming at the Toronto GC. Cumming had been trained as a clubmaker and greenkeeper at the Glasgow GC and came to Canada in 1900 from a club in the southwest of Scotland, where he had been the pro/greenkeeper. He lived at the course at the Toronto GC in a house provided by the club and he remained there for almost half a century. At first he was the head greenkeeper as well as the professional, and was assisted by a head groundsman. During his lifetime, George Cumming graduated numerous golf professionals and he also encouraged a few greenkeepers. Both Hawkins at Lakeview GC and later, William Chinery at York Downs GC were affected by their relationship with George Cumming. Besides being a professional and a greenkeeper, Cumming also laid out numerous golf courses during the early part of the century until the talented Stanley Thompson became the recognized expert on golf course architecture in Canada. That Cumming managed to win the 1905 Canadian Open attests to the fact that he was no mean golfer. When we read of his many accomplishments in *Golf In Canada: A History* by James Barclay, it leaves us wondering how one man could do so much during one lifetime.

When we examine George Cumming's credentials as a greenkeeper as described by Horace Hutchinson, the dean of the golf professionals again comes through with flying colors. In the early issues (1915) of *The Canadian Golfer*, George Cumming is a frequent contributor on the subject of greenkeeping and he generously makes some of the following recommendations and observations:

- *Every course should use compost made of soil mixed with manure or leaf mould.*
- *Prior to topdressing apply seed to the greens.*
- *Topdress in early September with a rich compost to stimulate growth on worn greens.*
- *Cummings favours seeding over sodding for it provides "a truer putting surface".*
- *Sodded greens are forever after rough and uneven.*
- *He advocates adding a bag of manure to irrigation water, almost a hundred years before the term fertigation was even invented.*

Cumming the greenkeeper had serious reservations about the function of green committees. "They may be experts in their own fields" exclaims Cumming, "but they know absolutely nothing about the science of greenkeeping. They are selected because they are good golfers and popular with their fellow members." These were all the wrong reasons according to Cumming and he laments the unwanted interference green committees often cause by stating flatly that: "Too many cooks spoil the broth."

It was not just George Cumming who served the dual role of professional and greenkeeper. Many other clubs followed the same practice as Toronto GC and some still do. Except that professionals long ago discovered that it was difficult to wear two hats, especially since greenkeeping was becoming ever more complex and time consuming.

Cumming meanwhile, with so much demand for his time, was getting tired of greenkeeping and at various times he tried to turn the reins over to William Sansom, the chief groundsman at Toronto GC. Except that Cumming never quite let go of the reins and Sansom was forever under the scrutinous eyes of the old golf pro. In spite of the professional interference, Sansom was to become one of the most prominent greenkeepers in all of Canada and even rose to serve as president of the National Greenkeepers Association of America. Cumming, technically his boss, never achieved those heights in the PGA.

# John Sutherland:
# The Best Greenkeeper in All of Canada

Before all that came to pass, we must look at what took place at other courses in the Dominion. One of the most prominent greenkeepers in Southern Ontario during the early part of the twentieth century was John Sutherland at the Hamilton GC. He became its greenkeeper in 1901 after a few years in a similar position at a Toronto course. Sutherland was an exceptional individual, much trusted and valued by the members at his club. When the Hamilton GC had to move to a new location, the directors instructed Sutherland, the Club's greenkeeper, and Nicol Thompson, the professional "to look over and inspect such properties as might be suitable for the purposes indicated and to gather such information as they could but taking care not to give out what the lands were to be used for." (From *One Hundred Years of Golf*, Hamilton GC Centennial Booklet.)

Sutherland was a man of quick action and what happened next is best described in his own words:

> *I had to travel then with a horse and buggy and I had to find suitable property on an electric or steam line because there were few automobiles in those days. I found a nice place between Hamilton and Waterdown but the CPR refused to stop at a golf course. I looked over the property later developed as the Dundas GC, but it was not until I ran into the postmaster at Ancaster one day that I began to get anywhere. He told me about this property we now have. Well, I drove out there one day with Mrs. Sutherland. The farm over 190 acres was owned by a widow and I sent Mrs. Sutherland in to ask the buying price and make other inquiries while I looked over the property and grabbed samples of the earth. It took two years of dickering to land the farm but it was what we wanted.*

*The Canadian Golfer* reports on the development of the Hamilton GC at Ancaster as follows:

> *When Harry Colt, the English architect, came to lay out the course in Ancaster, John Sutherland was on the grounds with him continuously. Before leaving, Mr. Colt informed the club's directors that the building of the course could not be in better hands than Sutherland's and that he was "as keen as mustard." The directors in turn never had any doubt as to the ability of their greenkeeper, but it was a satisfaction to have their opinion endorsed*

*by Mr. Colt. Anyone who has had to do with a new course knows something of the endless work. Superintendent Sutherland was busy directing such individual work as bridge building, laying drain and water pipe, cutting trees, blasting roots, draining swamps, ploughing land and sowing seeds. He was indefatigable.*

Sometime early in his greenkeeping days, Sutherland picked out of the ninth green a piece of sod, about a foot square, which he transferred to the nursery and which spread rapidly till it covered about two and a half acres. There were no weeds in this grass, which was of a velvet bent variety. The members at Hamilton GC suggested and unanimously agreed that this grass be named Sutherland Velvet Bent.

In 1937 John Sutherland requested partial retirement. It was arranged that he would stay on as groundsman in an advisory capacity and the position of superintendent of grounds was offered to his former assistant, Ed Walsh. Mr. Walsh accepted an annual salary of $1500. Sutherland continued at Ancaster for many more years. At Men's Opening Day in 1951, he was honoured for his 50 years of service to the club. He died in 1958. He was predeceased by his wife and son named Arthur (who had become a golf professional in the United States).

John Sutherland's interests were not limited to golf course maintenance. He laid out one new golf course in Ontario and helped establish the green for the Ancaster Bowling Club. According to his obituary in the local newspapers, he became known as one of the best greenkeepers in all of Canada.

Sutherland is fondly remembered at the Hamilton GC, but largely forgotten in the annals of greenkeeping in Ontario. Like so many before and since, he seems to have kept to himself and decided early on that his first priority was responsibility to his employer. We must thank Sutherland for setting high professional standards and being the forerunner in working as a team with the club's professional Nicol Thompson.

# Other Early Greenkeepers

William John Sansom was born in England in 1878 and immigrated to Canada at the turn of the century. His background was in gardening and he found employment at the Toronto GC working under the direction of George Cumming, who was then the most prominent pro/greenkeeper in Upper Canada. Sansom quickly advanced from being the gardener at Toronto Golf to becoming the head groundsman though still under the direction of George Cumming. Sometime before World War I, Sansom was appointed as chief greenkeeper.

At that time there were only a half dozen golf courses in the Toronto area and Toronto GC, being the oldest, was foremost among them. The club had a stable of 14 horses to pull its mowers and do other work. Horses needed to be taken care of every day of the week and Sunday was no exception. The greens staff took turns feeding the horses but the course was closed for play on the "Day of the Lord."

Care of the golf course was just as essential and Sansom explains that "in the early days we did not cut the greens so close. The heavy roller was very much in use. If a green did not putt true, the greenkeeper was instructed to give it a good rolling." Sansom soon discovered that heavy rollings were detrimental to the greens and he found that it was far better "to topdress with sharp sand or light, screened compost, well rubbed in." In that manner, the green could be made to putt smoothly without the soil becoming compacted. In the early days, bunkers and teeing grounds were more or less neglected.

Jim Hickman was another English gardener who immigrated to Canada and found work at the Beaconsfield GC near Montreal. Later, Hickman moved to the London Highland GC and was its greenkeeper for almost 50 years. He is best remembered for being the founder of the Western Ontario Greenkeepers Association.

John Gray was born in 1885 on a farm near Aberdeen, Scotland. In 1907 he immigrated to Canada and worked with architect Harry Colt in the Detroit area. In 1913 he supervised the construction of Essex GC near Windsor, Ontario. Then he went off to war, but missed all the action when he was assigned to train bag-pipers for the trench warfare.

## Grass in the Early Days

The North American conception of a fine sward of green grass at the turn of the century was often based on a typically English lawn of creeping bent, fescue, and bluegrasses. How did such lawns come about and how could they be created in America? The answer was simplistic: "First you level it, seed it and water it and then you roll it, for about 100 years." Few gardeners had the patience to make English lawns in America in that way. They looked for shortcuts and found them on the golf courses. Ever since golf began, the greenkeeper has been the resident expert on the establishment and maintenance of fine lawns as well as golf courses. Their livelihood depended on their ability to produce quality turf for the playing fields and there is no better motivation than economic necessity. Greenkeepers learned quickly that they had to be good to keep their jobs and in the process they became the experts in their field.

The early greens were seeded with a mixture of creeping bent mixed with equal parts of red fescue. The creeping bent was imported from Germany and became known as South German Bentgrass, what we would now call a Colonial Bentgrass species. With the outbreak of World War I, trade with Germany ceased and another source had to be found. Rhode Island Bentgrass became a satisfactory substitute.

With the prevailing methods of cutting the grass, regular watering, fertilizing, and aided by the warm summer temperatures, the fescue soon disappeared from the mix. By around 1900, greens consisted mostly of Colonial Bentgrass with the omnipresent Poa annua germinating naturally to form the turf. The greens were frequently quite rough for lack of regular cutting. The early greenkeepers protected the grass at the expense of the requirements of the game. With time they would learn that daily cutting at a lower height did not spell disaster for the turf. But the age-old conflict between what's good for golf and what's good for grass was discovered very early in the establishment of the game. To this day, that enigma has never been resolved satisfactorily to please both ardent golfers and professional superintendents.

Dr. Walter Harban on the Green Committee at the Columbia GC near Washington, D.C. stated in 1911, "For years it was impossible to get a greenkeeper to cut the greens close in the summer. After much insistence and finally absolute demand, the greens were cut not only every day, but very close. The improvement was so marked in quality, texture and strength of grass after the hot weather was over that the greenkeeper now resents the suggestion even to let them go for a day."

Dr. Harban further advises "to get the surface of your greens true by heavy rolling in early spring, followed afterward by frequent light rolling with the wooden roller." Dr. Harban did not live to see the stimp meter but if he had, he would have loved it. But long before the invention of the speed stick, the roller was one of the most important green-keeping tools.

In Both Canada and the United States the green committee had become all powerful and the chairman of the committee was almost as important in club's hierarchy as the captain. Whereas the committee members may have known a thing or two about golf, they knew absolutely nothing about the culture of golf course grass. The most important book about golf course maintenance was not published until 1917. Prior to that date, its author, Dr. Piper, had already become established as an authority on the subject. The need for qualified green-keepers became more pressing as the game of golf grew in popularity and the maintenance of fine turf became more complex. Yet, the profession was still in its infancy.

## Three Eras of Greenkeeping

According to Fred Hawkins, longtime greenkeeper at the Lakeview GC, the early days of greenkeeping can be divided into three distinct stages and since there are no higher authorities, we gladly accept the revered opinions of our esteemed colleague: the era of single horse machine or the pony mower, the triple cut machine era, and the era of the tractor.

1. *In the single horse era, Hawkins states that: "All the implements they had was one single horse machine, three hand machines to cut the greens, one team of horses with two barrels on a wagon and a handpump to water the greens when necessary and two heavy rollers. In the summer when the grass was growing good, they turned about 200 sheep loose on the course to help the one-horse machine. After a spell of wet weather, it seemed a race between the sheep making holes in the wet fairways and a steam roller rolling them out."*

SUSAN DUNLOP

There was, however, one exception to not using iron clubs with the feathery. Fairways in the 19th century had to be watered by horse and cart – a mobile sprinkler system – and mowed with a horse-drawn machine. To protect the fairway, horses were sometimes shod with large leather shoes; but there was no way of protecting against the relatively narrow, iron-shod wheels of the carts; consequently, these invariably left a fairly deep track in the grass. Since the balls frequently ended up in these ruts, an iron club, known as a "track" club, was produced for just this purpose: to dig the ball out and get it back into a more playable lie. The head of the "track" club was large, deep and heavy. Presumably, to avoid damaging the ball, the golfer attempted to take a sizeable divot by hitting well behind it.

*Printed from publication,* Victoria Golf Club 1893–1993, One Hundred Treasured Years of Golf.

2. *As golf became more popular, we enter the triple cut machine era: a single horse pulling a three gang set of gang mowers. Many new courses were built and more attention was paid to the construction of the greens. Instead of working the greens up out of old sod, they were slightly shaped and a few bunkers put in and the greens sodded with some of the finer grass mixtures. Play demanded closer putting surfaces. Water systems were installed for the greens and fairway mowers were made in gangs of three instead of one but still drawn by a single horse.*

3. *Now comes the era of the tractor. The greens have become boldly molded and heavily bunkered. The putting surfaces are seeded with one of the fine grasses instead of a mixture of bent and fescue or are put down with bent stolons. The size of greens increases from 3000-4000 sq. ft. to over 10,000 sq. ft. Tractors that started with three fairway gangs have increased*

*to five and even seven. Fairway watering systems have become common on most new courses.*

Hawkins's arbitrary division of the three different eras of greenkeeping corresponds roughly to the end of the first era leading up to the turn of century. The second era covers the time period leading up to the end of World War I. The era of the tractor takes us up to World War II. There is, of course, plenty of overlap at different courses in various parts of the country. Some courses kept horses well into the 1930s. Others used sheep to graze their fairways in the early part of the twentieth century. It is clear that the development of golf courses was on the move.

## The Bible of Greenkeeping

When Dr. Piper's book, *Turf for Golf Courses* was published in 1917, scientific greenkeeping became the order of the day and green committees and green chairmen realized that they needed better qualified greenkeepers and that golf professionals who doubled as greenkeepers would no longer do. Dr. Piper's book was a giant step forward but in terms of today's knowledge, his recommendations are taken with a grain of salt and bring faint smiles to our faces. Dr. Piper's remedies for turf problems are very primitive in today's terms, but at the beginning of the century that's all the knowledge that was available.

## Greenkeeping Remedies for Putting Greens in 1916

CRABGRASS—pluck it.
CLOVER—cut it out.

DANDELION—gasoline injected into the crown.

PLANTAIN—dig it out.

MOLES—trap with the harpoon trap.

FIELD MICE—poison with strychnine mixed with crushed wheat.

EARTHWORMS—
dilute bichloride of mercury in water; use as a spray.

ANTS—Inject carbon bisulfide with an oil spout.

GRUBS—push a ¼″ rod into the opening and spear the grub.

(From *Turf for Golf Courses* by Piper and Oakley. Note that none of the fungus diseases are even mentioned as problems on putting greens).

# Qualifications for Greenkeepers (circa 1910)

Hugh Wilson, Green Chairman at the Merion GC in Philadelphia, PA, offers his opinion on the requirements for a greenkeeper in the era prior to World War I and emphasizes the need for a budget:

*We have found that a greenkeeper should be a man who can diagnose any trouble quickly and who will nurse the grass with infinite care. He must watch the course every day and practically all day as changes come very rapidly in turf. One of the greatest failings of greenkeepers is due to the lack of thought on the part of the committees. They have never taught them thoroughly the question of cost. After careful study, one of committee members has worked out a budget which shows the detailed cost of the work month by month for the whole year. Of course this cannot be adhered to in every detail* *but the main object is to put the plan before the green-keeper so that he can see just what he has to do and how much money he has to do it with. It is most important to make the greenkeeper think in dollars and cents. The usual answer to a question of, 'Do you think you can do this?' will be 'Oh yes, it is not a very big job.' But if you ask the same man what it would cost, it would be hard for him to give an answer. The cost of mowing fairways and greens in addition to all the general cost, becomes an interesting and most profitable study. It is a very simple matter for the greenkeeper to keep track of the cost of a new bunker or the sodding of a green, and each time he does it, he learns a little more about the cost question and why it is such an important factor in all work. It also gives the greenkeeper a new interest in the work and a basis for comparison. We believe that you will find that a greenkeeper is keener for knowing that the last bunker cost $20.80 to build and the next one will cost a little less because he figured out a way to do it more cheaply. We have obtained splendid results by sending our greenkeeper to as many courses as possible in order that he may see what other persons are doing and profit by their good results as well as by their errors.*

This is foretold of things to come: meetings with other greenkeepers and the formation of greenkeeping associations, conferences and machinery exhibitions.

A temporary setback occurred with the outbreak of World War I, the war to end all wars, in Europe. Men were needed for the fronts and for the factories and there were cutbacks in the staffing of golf courses. Some golf courses even experimented with employing young women on the greens crew (Beaumaris GC, 1917). Others reverted back to sheep in

*A Sheep scene at Rosedale. Well–known Toronto club has over 100 sheep pasturing on its course. Rosedale members were proud of their "Ba Ba Boys." They will be kept over the winter and sold with the lambs in the spring. The venture has proved a great success. Provided by RCGA.*

an effort to cut cost and many courses turned excess land into the production of vegetables (such as potatoes and beans) to help with the war effort.

Some greenkeepers and golf professionals went to war. John Gray from Windsor Essex joined the 241st Canadian Scottish Battalion as a piper and went overseas to train others. So did Karl Keffer, the popular professional/greenkeeper at the Royal Ottawa GC who had twice won the Canadian Open. He soon became Corporal Keffer and was stationed overseas. Ever the golfer, Keffer played many of the famous courses in England and Scotland and was overwhelmed by the fine condition of the smooth greens. Change was in the wind and golf in Canada would never be the same when the war ended.

# *Historical Notes*

1873 Golf is first played in Canada in an organized fashion on Fletcher's Field in Montreal.

1875 The Quebec City GC is formed on the Plains of Abraham.

1880 Formation of the Brantford GC.

1880 The Montreal GC hires Mr. McNulty, the first grounds-man in Canada.

1881 The Montreal GC appoints William F. Davis as its first professional/greenkeeper.

1881 The birth of Toronto GC.

1881 Golf comes to Niagara-on-the-Lake and the Niagara GC is founded.

1888 Formation of the first golf club in the U.S. at Yonkers, New York.

In quick succession the following golf clubs were established—The Kingston GC (1888), Royal Ottawa (1891), Vancouver GC (1892), Rosedale GC (1893), a second club in Toronto, Victoria GC (1893), Winnipeg GC (1894).

1895 Formation of the RCGA and the first Canadian Amateur Championship.

The birth of the Edmonton GC (1896), and the Halifax GC (1896), Calgary CC (1897), and the Toronto Hunt Club (1897).

1899 Formation of the Regina GC. By the turn of the century there are now 50 golf clubs in Canada.

1904 First Canadian Open won by John Oke.

1904 Canadian Amateur golfer George Lyon wins the gold medal in golf at the St. Louis Olympics.

1914 The first public GC is opened in Edmonton Alberta.

1915 First issue of *The Canadian Golfer*, published in Brantford, Ont.

SUSAN DUNLOP

Horse-drawn mower.

*Printed from publication,* Victoria Golf Club 1893–1993, One Hundred Treasured Years of Golf.

1915 Mr. W. Lanigan becomes the first Green Chairman at St. Charles GC, Winnipeg

1916 The Quebec GC's chief greenkeeper dies in the line of duty. His death is reported in *The Canadian Golfer*. The nameless greenkeeper fell into the Montmorency River and was swept away in the current. Later his body was found at the bottom of the falls.

1916 Shawnee Mower Co. begins manufacturing of its one-horse mower in Montreal.

1917 Waterloo GC opens for golf on Sundays.

1917 The manager at the Rosedale buys 100 sheep at the Toronto Stock Yards to graze on the fairways. The sheep are fattened, shorn, and sold in the fall. Next year the flock is increased to 120. Thereafter, the experiment is abandoned and the manager once more concentrates on food and beverage.

1917 Rosedale spends $16,000 on stream bank stabilization.

1918 Stanley Thompson is promoted to Lieutenant at Headquarters Staff in France, and later returns to Canada and commences a successful career in golf course architecture in Canada and abroad.

# CHAPTER 11

# Between the Wars, the Roaring Twenties and the Great Depression

On the 11th hour of the 11th day of the 11th month in 1918, the warring factions in Europe laid down their arms and the soldiers returned home to Canada and to America. Karl Keffer came back to Royal Ottawa to relieve his wife who had been keeping shop during his absence. Keffer regaled anyone who would listen about the great golf courses in Scotland and England on which he had played. He was particularly impressed with the smoothness of the British greens. Keffer, who had won the Canadian Open twice before the war, was a voice in golf to be listened to, and his comments led to improvements on Canadian courses.

John Gray, the greenkeeper at Essex GC near Windsor, not surprisingly survived the war because he spent most of his time overseas in London teaching the art of piping. His stu-

# WORTHINGTON LAWN MOWERS AND TRACTORS

MADE IN CANADA

This 7 Gang 1936 model is equipped with the Worthington patented spring, adjustible to a maximum of 40 lbs and holds back of Unit to the ground ensuring a smooth cut under all conditions, and without adding to the draft.

Canadian
Distributor
**JOHN C. RUSSELL**
132 St. Peter St.,
Montreal, Que.

*Provided by RCGA.*

dents were quickly sent to the trenches in France and Flanders and many were not nearly as lucky as their teacher. Upon his return to Canada, Gray immediately got back in the swing of things at his home course near Windsor. Before long, he was called away to help rebuild a course for Scottish architect Donald Ross. That experience stood him in good stead when, a few years later, he was needed to build a new course for the members at Essex. It was to be another Donald Ross design.

Stanley Thompson, who just before the war's end had been promoted to Lieutenant in the Canadian Expeditionary Force, came back to Toronto and joined a partnership with his brother Nicol Thompson and George Cumming to design and construct golf courses. For Nicol Thompson and George Cumming, laying out golf courses was a part-time avocation since they were full-time professionals at their respective

*New 17th green under construction, Lakeview Country Club, Toronto, Canada—Herbert Strong, Architect.* The Canadian Golfer, *March 1921.*

clubs. For Stanley Thompson, who had an established reputation as an amateur golfer, designing and building golf courses quickly became a full-time occupation. In short order, he was in business for himself and business was booming. Just a few years after his soldiering days in France, he had some good projects underway and quickly gained recognition as a talented designer. In 1922 he advertised for "eight golf course superintendents" in the pages of *The Canadian Golfer*. It may have been the first time that greenkeepers were referred to as superintendents and it would take at least another half century before that term became generally accepted. Certainly, the greenkeepers had a friend in Stanley Thompson. In many instances, Thompson trained and graduated the men who helped him build new courses. Often, the best man was left behind as the superintendent to take care of the course that the master had created. Such appointments were mutually beneficial since Thompson was guaranteed that his creation would be well maintained and the new greenkeeper benefited from having a renowned architect as his sponsor.

Stanley Thompson created golf courses from coast to coast in Canada and also beyond its borders. Some of those courses are still highly ranked, such as Cape Breton Highlands, Capilano in Vancouver, and St. George's in Toronto. The two golf courses that brought Thompson the most fame were the Banff and Jasper courses in Alberta. Both courses were frequented by the rich and the famous and helped establish Thompson as one of the foremost architects in North America.

Golf was booming and any town or city worthy of the name had at least one golf course (and sometimes several) to accommodate all the citizens anxious to take up the new game. One exception was Chatham, Ontario. In June of 1918, *The Canadian Golfer* proclaimed CHATHAM, THE ONLY CITY IN CANADA WITHOUT A GOLF COURSE! To do something about this oversight of major proportions, George Cumming traveled to Chatham and informed the citizens that the land that they had chosen was suitable for "a first class 9- or 18-hole golf course." And thus Chatham joined the golf craze of the Roaring Twenties.

With golf being the craze of the 1920s, it is not surprising that greenkeeping also attracted the attention of Canadian golfers. Many of the golf professionals of that era still were looked upon as authorities on greenkeeping. Corporal Spittal, former Scarborough professional and just back from the war in Europe, expressed the following opinions:

- *It's poor fun to play of the same teeing ground from May till October. Tees should be enlarged and grassed.*
- *In some cases the green-keeper and the professional are "butting up" against one another!*
- *If the professional is of long experience, the green-keeper should look to him for advice.*

And Spittal proceeds to give plenty of advice:

- *Don't wait for a rainy day to fix your putting greens! That rainy day will fix the fairway but not the putting greens. Instead, keep the hose on the putting greens.*
- *Switch your greens well before you cut and roll them. Supposedly with a "biesum", a bundle of twigs tied together and to a handle.*
- *When cutting weeds from a green, cut them deep and place a few seeds in the cavity.*
- *Don't neglect the approaches to the greens. An old mowing machine will come in handy for that purchase.*
- *Don't leave the teeing box for a whole week in the same spot.*
- *Dress the fairway where it needs patching with a sprinkling of seed and dressing.*

Spittal also offered advice for his fellow golfers:

- *If you hook or slice into the rough, don't blame the Greenkeeper for not having that part of the course the same as the fairway. The rough is meant to be there.*
- *If you are playing a mashie shot to a blind hole and you send your caddie up the hill to give the line, don't forget to replace the turf yourself.*

Divots, of course, were hardly much of a problem in the days of hickory shafted clubs. Golfers hit the balls cautiously in early times before the steel shaft was introduced in 1920. They were always aware of breaking the shaft or even the club head on hard ground. Repairs were costly and inconvenient.

Problems were not just limited to greenkeeping technology. J. S. Redman, the professional and greenkeeper at the 18-hole Beaumaris GC in Muskoka, had been "up against it" in securing suitable labor for his links. He solved the problem in a unique way: He hired women! "Four golferettes looked after the Beaumaris course and looked after it mighty well." The girls in "natty costumes drove the mowers, trundled the rollers and generally looked after the links in a manner most adept." The chief greenkeeper reported that the golferettes in many respects were superior to mere men. It was the summer of 1919, long before feminism had even been thought of. (Heck, women did not even have the right to vote at that time!)

Meanwhile, Spittal and Redman were not the only experts on matters pertaining to greenkeeping. James Skinner, for many years the professional and greenkeeper at the Galt CC, had moved to St. Andrews NB and the Algonquin GC where he quickly became established as the local expert. That same year, 1921, Skinner advertised in *The Canadian Golfer* as a "Golf Architect and Turf Expert." We don't know of any golf courses laid out by Skinner, but most certainly he gave plenty of advice to area golf courses as well as keeping the members and guests happy at St. Andrews.

One of Canada's earliest greenkeepers, John Sutherland at the Hamilton GC, needed very little advice from the golf professionals. He was firmly established at the Colt-designed course that was built under Sutherland's supervision and he was recognized as an expert by his peers. In what may have been one the earliest professional endorsements, Sutherland lent his name to one of the first golf course tractors. A Hamilton car dealer converted a Ford automobile into a tractor capable of pulling grass cutters and "different golf club vehicles." Did Sutherland receive a royalty for the endorsement? We'll never know, but chances are the Hamilton GC received a healthy discount for being the guinea pig in trying out this newfangled rig.

## "Better Than Two Horses"
### At the Same Time Greatly Reducing the Cost

The above photograph was taken on the links of the Hamilton Golf and Country Club, Ancaster, Ont. It represents a FORD car specially constructed for towing grass cutters, but adaptable for towing all the different Golf Club vehicles.

John Sutherland, Green Keeper of the Hamilton Golf and Country Club, one of the continent's acknowledged experts, writes:

"The Ford car which the Universal Motors Limited of Hamilton, Ont. rebuilt to take care of our grass cutters has proven itself a phenomenal success, so much so, in fact, that we have had them build another one which is now in use. Not only do these two cars tow our Shawnee triplex cutters up our hills with ease, but one does as much work as two horse drawn vehicles at a greatly reduced cost. The average consumption of gas being about 4 to 6 gallons for a ten hour working day."

For particulars as to delivery and prices, write

### Universal Motors  Hamilton Limited
135 King Street West  :  Hamilton, Ont.

*First endorsement by a golf course superintendent.*

At Ontario's oldest golf club, the Toronto GC, a significant change had taken place. The club hired Fred Armitage as its Secretary/Manager. Prior to his appointment, Armitage had held a similar position across the street at the Lakeview course. Armitage would remain at Toronto GC for more than 40 years.

During that time he established himself both as a stern taskmaster for the staff and as an efficient administrator of the club's affairs.

William Sansom, born in England in 1878, immigrated to Canada at the turn of the century. He had a background in gardening and found employment at the Toronto GC. He quickly advanced from gardening to greenkeeping and as George Cumming's extracurricular activities increased, Sansom assumed more and more responsibility on the golf course.

*W.J. Sansom. Reprinted from* Greenmaster, *Sept/Oct 1974.*

In or about 1915, he became Head Greenkeeper but never escaped the dominating influence of both Fred Armitage and George Cumming during his years at Toronto Golf. In the *History of the Toronto Golf Club* (1876-1976), many pages are devoted to the contributions made by both Cumming and Armitage, but Sansom's name is never mentioned even once. In spite of his lack of recognition at his home course and probably because of his affiliation with the Toronto GC, Sansom was well known in the ranks of Toronto area greenkeepers. But an organization for greenkeepers in the province was still a few years away.

The Canadian Professional Golfers Association was first off the mark in becoming organized. That happy event took place in 1911. George Cumming and Karl Keffer were the principal forces behind the movement and Keffer remained the guiding light of the CPGA for the first quarter century of its existence.

In the fall of 1922, the club secretaries called a meeting at the city offices of the Summit GC in Toronto. It was attended by representatives from eight clubs and an organization was formed. E. Mason from the Lambton Club became the group's first president. F. Doran from the Summit Club was made the first secretary/treasurer; he was considered the "father" of the movement. Also in attendance were Bowyer from Rosedale, Thomas Fisher from Weston, and E. Trowell from the Hunt Club. Fred Armitage from the Toronto GC sent his regrets as did MacAlpine, recently appointed as secretary at the Lakeview GC. The purpose of the new association was quite lofty: "disseminating valuable information and an interchange of experience." They also had another, more down-to-earth goal and that was the improvement of course conditioning in the province. Many golf professionals had given up their role as greenkeepers and the secretaries soon realized that maintenance on the courses was beyond their scope as well.

In the summer of 1922, Dr. Piper came to Toronto and brought along a sod of bentgrass that he had lifted from the Washington GC. The sod was propagated in the nursery of the Toronto GC. Sansom shredded the stolons and within a short time he had enough for the greens at his course. Weston GC followed the same procedure to introduce creeping bentgrass to their greens. Prior to Dr. Piper's gift of grass to Ontario, the predominant turf on greens had been a mixture of fescue and Colonial Bentgrass as was used in Scotland and England on the links side golf courses. Fescue on greens had never been very successful because of our warm summers.

The introduction of stolonized Washington Bentgrass was

*Greens crew at Scarborough Golf Club 1922–23 behind the 17th Green. George Butler (father of Bryce Butler who provided picture) is in picture.*

a monumental turn of events. From 1922 until the introduction of Penncross and the demise of C-15 Bentgrass at Glenn abbey, stolonizing greens was the accepted method to establish putting greens. As with all milestones in history, not everyone suddenly abandoned old practices in favour of the new one. For many years after the introduction of Washington Bentgrass, greens in Canada were still seeded with grass seed from Prince Edward Island, from Germany, and even from New Zealand. Noted golf course architect Geoffrey Cornish states that Scottish immigrants who had settled in Prince Edward Island decided that they needed to move and departed for New Zealand. Upon their arrival in New Zealand, they emptied their mattresses stuffed with bentgrass hay. The bentgrass flourished and soon the farmers were harvesting the seed for North American and European lawns. In the meantime, farmers on Prince Edward Island undertook to harvest bentgrass seed. Hence, Prince Edward Island Bentgrass and New Zealand Brown Top are the same grass. Seed in New Zealand was grown in plots which allowed for quality control, whereas most seed from Prince Edward Island came from pastures and hayfields. Although more expensive, New Zealand Brown Top was favoured by greenkeepers and architects alike. That is, until they discovered stolonized bent, more particularly Washington Bent as introduced by Dr. Piper.

*Charles Vancouver Piper,*
*1867–1926. Reprinted from*
The Canadian Golfer.

Not only did Dr. Piper advocate better quality grasses for our putting greens, he also encouraged greenkeepers to become organized as the professionals had done. Dr. Piper realized that better golfing conditions could be achieved only by the efforts of better informed greenkeepers. He emphasized the need for turfgrass research at state colleges in the U.S.A. and at our own Ontario agricultural colleges. Greenkeepers in the field needed the backing of science and technology. Again, with the urging of Dr. Piper, the RCGA established a green section similar to its USGA counterpart, though on a much smaller scale. In 1924, the RCGA appointed C. A. Tregillus as its first manager of the Green Section. For a number of years, he would write technical articles about golf course maintenance in the pages of *The Canadian Golfer* until he moved to the United States.

The stage was set for the founding of a greenkeeping association. But it was a manager, and not a greenkeeper, who took the bull by the horns and made the inspirational first move. During the late summer of 1924, C. L. Knuth secretary/manager at the Weston GC, sent out letters to the greenkeepers in the greater Toronto area and invited them to an inaugural meeting at his club. Knuth had obtained a set of the by-laws of the Golf Greenkeepers Association of England and it was Knuth's intention to pattern the new Canadian group on its English forbears. To ensure a good turnout, Knuth had the invitation reprinted in the August issue of *The Canadian Golfer.*

The attendance at the October 4 meeting at Weston GC was not overwhelming, but it was sufficient to make an auspicious start. The following is an alphabetical list of all those in attendance:

1. Abbott, John, greenkeeper
2. Cameron, John, greenkeeper, Weston GC
3. Carter, C., C. I. L. Sales Manager
4. Dunlop, J. M., unknown affiliation
5. Fordyce, J., greenkeeper
6. Freeman, Chris, greenkeeper, Toronto Hunt
7. Hawkins, Bert, greenkeeper, Lake View GC
8. Kirby, William, greenkeeper, Lambton GC
9. Knuth, C. H., Manager, Weston GC
10. Mason, F., Secretary, Lambton GC
11. McAlpine, J., Secretary, Lake View GC
12. Perrin, unknown affiliation
13. Ray, W.E., unknown affiliation
14. Robinson, Charles, greenkeeper, Thistletown GC
15. Sansom, William, greenkeeper, Toronto GC

These 15 men represented nine Toronto area clubs as well as Hamilton and Glendale golf clubs. The meeting was presided over by Fred Mason but he quickly made a motion (seconded

*Canadian Golf Greenkeepers Association. Meeting at Weston Golf Club, Oct. 4ᵗʰ, 1924.*

by Fred Hawkins) to the effect that William Sansom be appointed Chairman and the latter just as quickly moved (seconded by Charles Robertson) that Fred Hawkins be the secretary of the organizing committee. It was further decided that a second meeting of the new association was to be held at the Prince George Hotel in Toronto on Wednesday, November 11 to elect permanent officers and committees.

It certainly appears from reading between the lines that some fancy footwork had taken place prior to the meeting to make sure that Sansom and Hawkins would take charge of the new group. They did this with the help of some of the secretaries, not only for the next meeting, but for the next 15 years! Surprisingly, the new group called itself the Canadian Golf Greenkeepers Association, a somewhat premature move. Shortly after the initial euphoria, reality set in when the greenkeepers applied for a federal charter. They discovered that the cost of incorporation in the province of Ontario was much less than that of the Dominion and, being thrifty, opted for the less expensive alternative.

While secretaries and managers constituted almost half of those in attendance at the Weston meeting, a month later at the

Prince George Hotel, only greenkeepers were present. In an unusual move the new association appointed an Honorary President and an Honorary Vice President, respectively, S. B. Gundy and Professor Clarke with the Department of Agriculture in Ottawa. Gundy was a past president of the RCGA and a member at Rosedale. Both were men of substance in their respective fields which gave the young association instant credibility.

The appointments or elections (we are not sure which) of Sansom and Hawkins were reaffirmed and the following were registered as charter members:

John Anderson, Scarborough GC
James Scotland, Scarborough GC
I. McCallum, Scarborough GC
John Cameron, Weston GC
William Gray, Lakeshore GC
Chris Freeman, Toronto Hunt
Malcolm Bunting, Glendale GC
James Hickman, London Highland GC
Horne, Welland GC
Art Nixey, London Hunt
Jim Stanfield, Mississaugua GC

The association adopted a constitution based on a document that had been sent over from England and manager Knuth at Weston had used as the starting point for the October 4 meeting. Sansom and Hawkins outlined an ambitious set of goals for the new group:

- *Mutual self-help*
- *Improvement of its members*
- *Competitions*
- *Prizes for essays, drawings, and models of greens and bunkers*

- *A benevolent fund for the relief of deserving members*
- *An agency for obtaining employment*

Membership was limited to greenkeepers, greenkeepers' assistants, and in the case of professionals who combine work on the course with instruction, the head groundsman. This stipulation was an obvious effort to elevate groundsmen to become greenkeepers and also a bit of a snub to the pro/greenkeepers who in any case already had their own association— the PGA. The new group set an entrance fee at $2.00 and annual dues at $10.00. Later, the entrance fee would be eliminated and the dues reduced to half that amount for the simple reason that new members were not exactly lining up to join.

Sansom laid out a plan for the new association that included winter meetings with lectures by experts and summer meetings at golf courses. Both Sansom and Hawkins were brought up in the horse and buggy era and neither ever learned how to drive an automobile. For transportation they relied on trains for long-distance trips and for shorter hauls, friends or relatives drove them. Bert Sansom, the son of the founder, who had worked in the pro shop at Toronto GC, recalls driving his father and Bert Hawkins to winter meetings in Toronto. The return trip to Port Credit was often quite lively with the pair singing in the backseat, no doubt from too much "meeting" at the Royal York Hotel. In spite of the difficulties of transportation, the new association got off the ground successfully. William Sansom, Bert Hawkins, Charlie Robinson, Albert Horne, John Cameron, and Malcolm Bunting duly signed the letters of incorporation. It seems a peculiar coincidence that Cameron from the Weston GC should be a signatory. More than 40 years later, Bill Forrester, his successor at Weston, signed the letters of incorporation for the Canadian Golf Superintendents Association.

In an article written in 1931, Sansom states that an executive committee was appointed in 1924 and "that it has remained the same." The members of the committee were: Harold Lloyd from Rosedale; I. McCallum, Scarborough; William Kirby, Lambton; Chris Freeman, Hunt Club; and Jack Stanfield; Mississaugua. Howard Lloyd, nicknamed "Smiling Dad" because he was older and always exhibited a broad smile, became good friends with Bill Sansom. Strangely, he did not attend the first two meetings, but became quite active until his untimely death in 1933.

South of the border, greenkeepers had become equally restless and were just as anxious to become organized as their Canadian counterparts. The Ohio group was first off the mark. It became established in April 1923, followed by the Greenkeepers Club of New England in February 1924. The Ontario Association is therefore the third oldest association, but the first independent group, since both the Ohio association and the New England group were chaired by greens chairmen. (Obviously, the Americans lacked confidence initially, which the Ontarions did not).

In Ohio, John Morley, the greenkeeper at the Youngstown GC near Cleveland, spent much of his spare time visiting golf courses and meeting with fellow greenkeepers. This led to the formation of the National Greenkeepers Association at the Sylvania GC in Toledo, Ohio on September 13, 1926. There were no Canadians present at this meeting, but at the 1927 winter conference in Chicago, John Gray is clearly recognizable in the second row of a group photograph. Gray was one of the first Charter Members of the NGA. Other early participants were Sansom and Hawkins. In 1927, Bert Hawkins is listed as one of 14 vice-presidents of the National Association of Greenkeepers of America. Although the appointment was short-lived, it proves the Canadian involvement with the American association from the start.

—⚎—

# Note of Sadness

From *The Canadian Golfer*, February 1926:

> *Dr. Charles Vancouver Piper passed away suddenly in Washington, D.C. on February 13th. He had been in poor health for some time. In 1919 Dr. Piper had discovered a clump of bentgrass growing on a green at the Washington Golf and Country Club. By vegetative propagation he secured a quantity of roots of this grass and in 1921 distributed the stolons to various golf courses for trial. The grass became known as Washington Creeping Bentgrass and was used on hundreds of courses throughout the U.S.A. and Canada. Dr Piper was chairman of the USGA Green Committee and was largely responsible for their monthly publication. Dr. Piper also introduced Sudan grass to America and promoted the establishment of soybeans.*
>
> *He was born in Victoria, BC on June 16, 1867, the same year that Canada became a nation. After initial schooling in Canada, he received his education in botany at the University of Washington and later moved the U.S. Department of Agriculture from where it was a short step to the U.S. Golfing Association.*

# The New Association

During the next few years, the new Ontario association struggled for survival. In 1928, it organized a successful Field Day at the Rosedale GC, but it was not until the end of the decade that the Ontario Greenkeepers Association was firmly entrenched.

In February 1929, Sansom gave a major address at the old Statler Hotel in Buffalo, NY, (a landmark to this day) to the assembled members of the National Greenkeepers Association. Colonel John Morley was the president and no doubt in the audience. Sansom begins by stating that "looking back 12–15 years, greenkeeping in Canada was in its infancy and the golf course was in most cases under the direct supervision of the professional." It is almost a certainty that Sansom is speaking of his personal experiences at the Toronto GC. George Cumming was still very much the boss on the golf course and Sansom also had to account to the stern Fred Armitage, club secretary.

# *Early Agronomics*

Preparing compost, according to Sansom, is the most important item in greenkeeping:

> *The dressing and preparing of compost should be carried out in a scientific manner. Make sure that the compost is light enough! To dress a green with anything like a heavy sticky nature is asking for trouble. Compost should be made at the very least one year before using. A green-keeper with a good supply of compost on hand, will always be an asset to any club.*

On rolling turf:

> *The heavy roller was very much in use in former days. If a green did not putt true, the greenkeeper was instructed to give number so and so a good rolling to true it up. There is*

*very little doubt that rolling too often and using too heavy a roller, especially on clay soils did much harm. I would say that in former days more greens were spoiled through over-rolling than from the want of it. If a green does not putt true, it is far better to give it a good topdressing of sharp sand or light, screened compost, and well rubbed in. Top-dressing with sharp sand at the end of the season is a good means of protecting the turf over winter.*

And now here, Sansom, the true greenkeeper, spoke straight from the heart about feeling with his feet:

*The moment one walks on a firm green, it is very easy to form an opinion from the feel of the turf whether its firmness is due to over-rolling or the correct method of top-dressing. In the latter case, there is nothing harsh about it, but the soil is porous as well as being firm. It is a pleasure to walk on such a green."*

Old Tom Morris would have been proud if he could have heard those words. The Scottish pro/greenkeeper (who had been dead for some time) was the first to advocate topdressing greens with sand and was a great advocate of firm greens. Sansom commented further on the rising expectations of post-war golfers:

*In the old order of things we did not cut our greens so close. Bunkers and teeing grounds were more or less neglected. Today the requirements are much more exacting. We find we have to cut the greens closer and almost daily (but not on Sundays!). Teeing grounds have to be kept in good shape by topdressing materials and divots replaced, and markers moved every day, clean towels put out at least three times per week, bunkers raked and groomed daily and many more details carried out which were not done formerly.*

In concluding his presentation, Sansom had this to say:

*In October of 1924 we organized our Local Greenkeepers Association. Our numbers are few and we enjoy the privilege of visiting the different courses for our summer meetings. In the winter months, we hold our monthly meetings inside.* [The greenkeepers often met outside in the summer. They were not always allowed inside the clubhouse. One of the first meetings the author attended at the York Downs Golf Club in 1958 was conducted on the front lawn of the clubhouse.] *We have become better acquainted and discuss our different ideas and exchange information. Some two years ago we became connected with the National (1927) Greenkeepers of America and we look forward to receiving our copy of the National Greenkeeper and to be present at the Annual Convention.*

*In conclusion, most greenkeepers have recognized the fact that there is much diversity of opinion on the subject of greenkeeping. Varying views have frequently been expressed. Practical knowledge teaches us to appreciate the fact that what may be quite right to do in one place maybe just the reverse in another.*

President Sansom is alluding to the fact that many of the wintertime discussions conducted at the Sons of England Hall under the influence of whiskey and beer often deteriorated with the widely diverging views being settled by harsh words and, at times, even fisticuffs. Eventually, the meetings were moved to the Royal York Hotel and, from time to time, the liquor supply was cut off. It is interesting to note that from the very start, these hardworking men held strong views and

*Sansom is in the center of the photograph, flanked by colleague Howard Lloyd the greenkeeper at Rosedale, and Professor Tomlinson. Next to Tomlinson is Charles Wright, the seed expert with the Dominion Government in Ottawa.*

often disagreed amongst themselves. Sansom tried to smooth the differences over by suggesting that what may work at one golf course often does not work at another, thus making it possible for all greenkeepers to be right all the time, at least on their own turf. Sansom the politician covered all bases and he was on his way. He was appointed to the executive committee and in 1934 he became president of NGA.

The summer preceding the big stock market crash found the Ontario greenkeepers attending a meeting at the Ontario Agricultural College in Guelph as guests of Professor Tomlinson. Also in attendance was Chuck Evans from Chicago, the great American golfer and the original designer of the Guelph

Cutten Club, the one and only course Evans laid out. This was the first of many meetings to follow in a long-standing, mutually beneficial relationship between the college and the greenkeepers: For many years to follow, the greenkeepers would trek to Guelph to learn the technical side of their profession.

In 1929, Sansom also attended the U.S. Open at Winged Foot GC. By that time he had been appointed as Vice President of the National Association of Greenkeepers. Upon his return he presented his observations to the Ontario Greenkeepers Association at the July meeting at the Mississaugua GC. Sansom was surprisingly candid in his observations. While he considered the American greens better than ours in terms of design and construction (because they were in many instances modern greens), for the very same reasons he stated that the turf on our greens was better, because they were older and "age alone produces turf." Some would consider this a 'dig' at his American colleagues to remind them that organized golf in Canada was at least 15 years older than in the U.S.

At the same meeting the members discussed the possibility of inviting the National Greenkeepers Association to conduct their midwinter convention in Toronto. No agreement was reached but the seed was planted. By the end of that year, Sansom and some of his colleagues prepared to attend the conference in Kentucky, a meeting at which John Morley was inaugurated as a Kentucky Colonel and became forever after known as Colonel Morley, a big name for a small man.

At this same Kentucky meeting, Sansom was once again on the podium. This time he talked about fertilizer and while he was far too cautious to recommend specific fertilizers, he stressed the need for plant food on greens where nutrients needed replenishment and on fairways where the grass competed with weeds. Sansom said: "Club Officials would do well to appropriate a sum of money each year for fertilizing fairways. When turf is thin and undernourished, weeds and clover will take possession—a sure sign of the absence of proper fertilizer." Sansom spoke from personal experience. The soil on his Toronto golf course was of a sandy nature and without adequate water and fertilizer, the turf had been less than adequate. The summer of 1929 was dry and hot and the golfers at the Toronto GC had been none too pleased with the condition of their fairways. But worse was yet to come.

The spring of 1930 was typical of the kind that strikes Southern Ontario about once every ten years. According to an article in the June issue of *The National Greenkeeper*, Eastern Canada experienced drought in October and November followed by a severe winter and a February thaw, which caused premature growth followed by yet another cold spell. When spring arrived, there was much dead grass on tees, greens, and fairways. Combined with the stock market crash the previous fall, there was little to cheer about for Canadian investors and golfers.

A brief few days of levity occurred in early summer with the Toronto visit of Colonel Morley and his executive committee of the National Greenkeepers Association. Their purpose was to check out Toronto as a potential National Conference site, and to ensure a proper impression of the city, the committee was housed at the prestigious Royal York Hotel. In addition to Colonel Morley, the American guests also included greenkeepers Fred Burkhardt from Cleveland, John Quaill from Pittsburgh, Louis Evans from Philadelphia, George Davies from Kentucky, Robert Hayes from New York, John MacGregor from Chicago, and Robert Power, the editor of *The National Greenkeeper*.

In addition to their busy meeting schedule, the Ameri-

*Provided by RCGA.*

cans found time to visit the following golf courses: Lakeview, Mississaugua, Islington, Lambton, Rosedale, Scarborough, and Cedarbrook. At Toronto Golf, the greenkeepers were hosted to a luncheon arranged by Fred Armitage and the Chairman of the Green Committee, F. J. Mulqueen. But their hospitality was not without its price; the fairways on the golf course were still in deplorable condition and the Toronto GC looked for answers from the assembled greenkeepers. They asked pointed questions, such as what should be done to restore the course to its former splendor. Most of the guests were too polite to answer, but John Quaill stated the situation succinctly: "They have a problem there as the topsoil is very sandy and they have many difficulties keeping the greens moist and also in holding the fertilizer in the soil as it leaches down through it very rapidly." Louis Evans of

# The Worthington Mower

**THE SHAWNEE TRIPLE MOWER—1923 MODEL**

Cuts a swath of eighty-six inches. "The spring's the thing" that prevents the revolving knives from jumping or "bobbing" over the surface. Used by practically all the leading clubs in Canada.

*IMMEDIATE SHIPMENT FROM MONTREAL STOCK.*
*Catalogue covering 1923 model on request.*

J. C. RUSSELL, Distributor,
109 Youville Square, Montreal

WORTHINGTON MOWER CO.,
Shawnee-on-Delaware, Pa.

*1924. Provided by RCGA.*

Philadelphia advocated a coarser sand and Robert Hayes of New York believed that peatmoss would provide the carpet, which could not be obtained under the prevailing conditions.

J. Evans, the golf editor of the *Toronto Globe* who attended the luncheon reported: "Out of the debate which became warmer as it proceeded, Mr. Mulqueen and Mr. Armitage secured opinions of value to improve a course, regarded from the point of view of attention paid to it, as the first in the Dominion."

Sansom wanted more fertilizer and an improved watering system. He got neither. The Americans concluded their stay in Toronto with a splendid banquet at the Old Mill on the Humber River (which is still a fine restaurant at the same location 70 years later). The banquet was sponsored by the Rice Lewis

Company and attended by 31 guests. Most of those in attendance were Ontario greenkeepers but there was also a delegation from the Buffalo area. This may have been the start of a long lasting relationship between the western New York group and the Ontario association, earmarked with many reciprocal visits in years to come.

Colonel Morley and some of his executives left the next day for Chicago and a meeting with the club managers and the professional golfers associations to discuss matters of mutual interest. Morley was small in stature, barely 5' 6". At about 135 lbs, he was as thin as a bunker rake. But what he lacked in size was made up for in bravado. Born in England, he had come to North America as a gardener and became a greenkeeper. More than anyone else, he was responsible for the birth of the National Greenkeepers Association and kept it going through its formative years. When the young association lost most of its money when its bank became insolvent, things looked bleak. Yet Morley was not about to let his brainchild die and the NGA survived with the help from many friends. In the golf course industry, Morley became recognized as one of the top greenkeepers of his era, not only in the United States, but also abroad. When George Clark, the commissioner of the Department of Agriculture in Ottawa, contacted Colonel Morley for information about creeping bents, Morley promptly shipped samples up to Winnipeg from the nursery on his course in Youngstown, Ohio. The turf had been developed by the ardent greenkeeper.

Words of wisdom by Colonel Morley in 1927:

- *It is the little things that we neglect that help to cause us so much trouble. The big things seem to take care of themselves.*

- *Don't do your experimenting on the putting greens or fairways. Do it on the nursery instead.*
- *How many veins are there in a blade of grass? You ought to know.*
- *When you know that you spend the club's money more economically than your own, you can realize that you are on a road leading to executive ability.*
- *One great trouble in life is that we always remember what we ought to forget.*
- *Let our membership be mellowed by good fellowship, humanized by charity and dedicated to service.*

In September of 1930, the greenkeepers held their second golf course machinery and supply exhibition at the Royal York Golf Club (now St. Georges). The date was carefully selected not to conflict with the Canadian National Exhibition. The planning paid off and the event was a resounding success. More than 200 attended, some from as faraway as Quebec. The list of exhibitors included the following:

- Rice Lewis & Sons (Pennsylvania Lawnmowers)
- Staude Tractors
- Sherwin Williams (Arsenate of Lead)
- Jacobson Power Mowers
- Hardie Sprayers
- Lark Golf Sprinklers
- Buckner Sprinklers
- Skinner Sprinklers
- Milorganite Fertilizers
- National Mower Company
- Wm. Rennie Seeds
- Steele Briggs Company
- C. I. L.
- Aikenhead Company

# The Golf Greenkeepers Association of Ontario

## W. J. SANSOM - President
### Toronto Golf Club

## H. HAWKINS - Sec.-Treasurer
### Lakeview Golf Club

## Executive Committee:

| | |
|---|---|
| H. LLOYD - - - | Rosedale Golf Club |
| W. KIRBY - - - | Lambton Golf Club |
| F. HAMM - - - | Royal York Golf Club |
| J. AUSTIN - - . | Humber Golf Club |
| J. STANFIELD - - | Mississauga Golf Club |
| C. W. FREEMAN - | Toronto Hunt Golf Club |
| A. McCALLUM - . | Scarboro Golf Club |
| J. ABBOT - - - | Islington Golf Club |
| J. ANDERSON - - - | Cedar Brook Golf Club |
| F. HAYNES - - - | Summit Golf Club |

*Equipment pamphlet, 1930, Golf Equipment Show.*

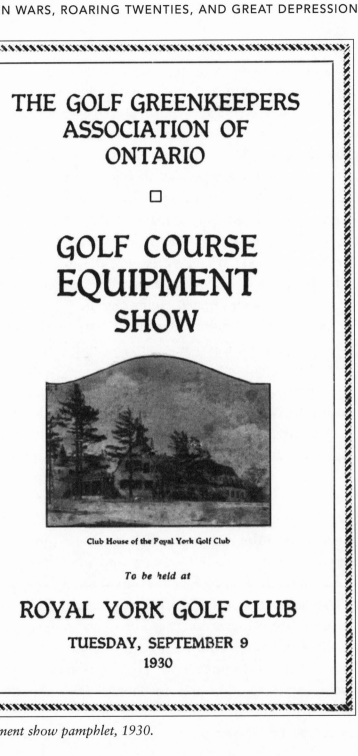

*Equipment show pamphlet, 1930.*

Aikenhead Company, hardware merchants in Toronto, had obtained the manufacturing rights for what must have been one of the most unusual pieces of equipment at the entire exhibit: the Ideal Triplex, which featured two giant rollers and three cutting units. This behemoth was advertised as being capable of cutting 15–40 acres of grass in a single day. The new mower was not a success, but in spite of this unfortunate adventure into the golf course industry, Aikenhead became a prosperous and thriving company. A third generation scion of the family served for a while on the Green Committee of the Toronto Board of Trade, overseeing the management of the golf courses. The hardware chain eventually became part of the giant American retailer, Home Depot.

A Quebec delegation attended the exhibition for the express purpose of discovering first hand how the Ontario greenkeepers had organized and how they were taking care of their courses. In an exchange between the two groups, it soon became apparent that in Quebec the primary purpose was to promote cooperative purchasing while the Ontario greenkeepers were interested foremost in the exchange of information at their monthly meetings. Some Quebec greenkeepers signed on as members of the Ontario association and agreed to meet again at some future date, but a chance to start a truly national association was lost. With Sansom soon to become president of the American group and many Ontario greenkeepers already holding membership in the American group, it was apparent that the Ontario boys were more interested in the close-by Americans than in their fellow Canadians stretched out across the length and breath of the Dominion. Thus while the promise of a possible relationship between Quebec and Ontario came to naught, the exhibition at the Royal York GC was a resounding success. Sansom and his committee of Hawkins, Lloyd, Austin, Kirby, Hamm, Stanfield, Freeman, McCallum, Abbot, Anderson, and Hayes raked up a substantial profit, which put the association on solid financial footing.

## Dark Clouds

But there were clouds on the horizon. Like the preceding summer, the summer of 1930 had been an exceedingly dry one with no appreciable rain since the beginning of May. Many golf courses were suffering, including, once again, President Sansom's home course. Sansom admitted that the fairways were burned in spots but he assured his committee that with the predictable arrival of fall rains, all would be well. It was not to be!

In 1931, the American Greenkeeping Convention took place in Columbus, Ohio and it was a happy occasion for Sansom. Not only was his star rising on the executive committee of the NGA, but with the help of his friend and colleague Howard Lloyd, the superintendent from Rosedale, he won a prize. A contest had been developed at the urging of Mr. Sansom which involved preparing a three-dimensional model of a golf hole. The idea garnered little support and Lloyd and Samsom won virtually by default, but it was a win nonetheless.

Sansom was in a buoyant mood. An early spring helped lift his spirits. In *The National Greenkeeper* spring issue, he said: "We should have our best season. There isn't anything to concern us. Not in many years have conditions been so consistently good". Just to be on the safe side, he recommended and endorsed the installation of a "hoseless watering system" on fairways and around greens. According to Sansom, such systems could be operated by just one man and thus save the club a lot of money. While nearby Lakeview had already installed such a system, Toronto GC lagged sadly behind. Sansom's fairways were again showing signs of lack of water and a proliferation of weeds had invaded the turf.

In a 1931 article in the *Golf Course Reporter*, Sansom discussed once more the formation of the Ontario Greenkeepers Association which gives us some valuable insight:

> *At the time of formation there were 11 members. That number has increased to 27 by 1931, all of whom also belong to the National Greenkeepers Assn. of America. The purpose of the organization was to advance the science of greenkeeping, maintain a closer fellowship among the greenkeepers of the district, accumulate practical knowledge on the problems of greenkeeping with a view to promoting more efficient and economical maintenance of golf courses and to serve as an agency through which members may obtain employment. We hold educational meetings from time to time in which specialists from the Agricultural College in Guelph assist. We also hold regular meetings during the summer on the various golf courses, at which discussions of turf problems yield very helpful results. The different clubs are very generous in providing us with a room and luncheon at these meetings. We are often called upon for advisory service, from which the smaller clubs especially profit. We are also asked for advice through the mail. And the inquiries are always given prompt attention. Our winter meetings are held at the Sons of England Hall on the second Tuesday of each month. These meetings are very helpful from an educational standpoint. A greenkeeper is invited to prepare a paper to be presented at the meeting, and this serves as a basis for discussion. We do not issue a publication of our own but the local papers and occa-*

*sionally* The Canadian Golfer *magazine lend publicity to our activities. Once in two years a machinery demonstration is held. As few of our greenkeepers play golf, we have not had occasion to hold any tournaments. Our membership is confined to greenkeepers and assistants but we strive to enlist the cooperation of green committees, secretary managers, professionals and stewards, as it is quite essential that all work in close touch for the best interest of the clubs.*

In 1932 at the Pennsylvania Hotel in New York, William Sansom once again became vice-president of the American association. Two years later in Pittsburgh he was elected president. Being in the limelight for Sansom was nothing new under the sun. He was often asked for his opinions and quoted in the newspapers. During the 1930-s when labour and union prob-

# TORO
## Putting Green Mower

**TORO Putting Green Mower**

—the only putting green mower that is completely equipped with ball-bearings (highest quality), positively protected from dust.

All cut gears operate in an absolutely oil-tight and dust-proof case. All working parts quickly accessible. It will push easier and cut smoother than any mower made. It will follow the contour of the surface without scalping the ground in going over ridges, insuring a nice, even clip on the undulated green.

It comes COMPLETE with Alemite greasing system, grass catcher box, and steel-wheeled, rubber-tired carrying cart,—no extras to buy. We believe that we can easily show you why this is the finest and most dependable putting green mower ever put into service. Write for full details of construction.

*Reprinted from* The Canadian Golfer, *May 1924.*

lems were commonplace, J. Evans, the golf editor of the *Toronto Globe* asked Sansom a pointed question about his association and Sansom snapped:

"In no sense can we be classified as a labour organization. Greenkeeping at present [1932] is something more than manual labour." That response was often to be repeated in years to come. From time to time, a small segment of the association's members wanted a more aggressive association. They were always turned down by the majority who agreed with the founding father that theirs was a professional association and not a labour union!

Meanwhile, neighboring Mississaugua was preparing for the Canadian Open under the direction of Jack Stanfield. The mild spring with reduced run-off was a bonus for Stanfield and reduced his labour load. The Credit River, which bisects the course, habitually overflowed its banks. It deposited silt and boulders on the fairways and made more work for Stanfield and his crew. Preparation for the Open had begun the preceding fall with an application of 30 tons of fertilizer followed by a similar amount the following spring. The kind of fertilizer is not specified, but in view of the huge quantity it seems likely to have been several applications of Milorganite, a relatively new product being promoted by a smart young agronomist from Milwaukee, O. J. Noer.

Supplying fertilizer to golf courses was becoming big business. In July, the Ontario greenkeepers were hosted by the CIL Company and toured the company's plant in Hamilton, Ontario. Everyone was suitably impressed and for all we know, the fertilizer that Stanfield applied to Mississaugua's fairways may even have been a CIL product.

The summer of 1931 was another hot and humid one with barely any change in temperatures between the day and nighttime highs. The heat spell lasted for more than five weeks and for the first time the turf was attacked by Brown Patch and the greenkeepers were almost powerless to combat the disease. Many courses suffered heavily as this new disease ran rampant, not only in Ontario, but also in Quebec. Eighteen greenkeepers attended a meeting at the Scarborough CC and were joined by three secretaries/managers. The latter attended specifically to learn more about the new disease, which was wreaking havoc with golf course turf. After an inspection of the Scarborough GC, all agreed (even the three managers), "that criticism could not be directed to the greenkeeper and that it was best to go to work and repair the damage." At the time the word "Dollar Spot" had not yet come into use. To describe the difference between Dollar Spot and Brown Patch, greenkeepers would refer to one as small brown patch and the other as large brown patch.

During the hot summer, Sansom and some other members of the greenkeepers association made many visits to courses in Ontario and they were able to "render valuable service to fellow greenkeepers who had encountered trouble." Sansom had taken a leaf out of Colonel Morley's book. Morley is alleged to have visited more than 200 golf courses during his professional life, all for the sake of helping his colleagues.

In September 1931, turf plots were established at the Royal York GC under the auspices of the RCGA and with the cooperation of the Dominion Department of Agriculture. Frank Hamm, the course superintendent, hosted a meeting that fall so his colleagues could inspect the plots. Bentgrasses and fescues were sown by seed or stolon. Seventy-two varieties and more than 10,000 square feet of ground were used for this purpose. The greenkeepers were apprehensive about the entire exercise. They had been promised so much by the RCGA and so little had been delivered. No wonder the

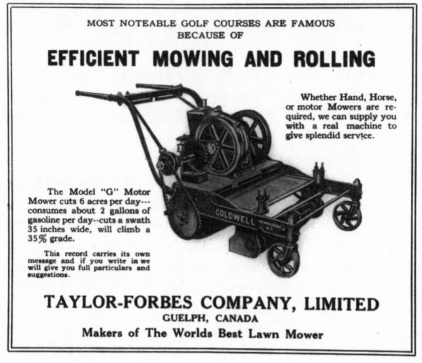

The Canadian Golfer, *Vol. VII, No. 12.*

greenkeepers were skeptical. Still, they examined the plots with open minds and decided to come back next year for another look.

The New Zealand trade commissioner made a visit to Toronto in the fall of 1931 and addressed a group of golfers at the exclusive Empire Club. Not surprisingly, no greenkeepers or superintendents were included in the audience. The purpose of this visit was to promote the sales of fescue grass seed to Canadian golf courses. The commissioner espoused the merits of fescue for fairways and greens, but it was already too late: Ontario greenkeepers had long ago switched over to stolonized bentgrass. Dr. Piper had seen to that when he brought a sod of Washington Bentgrass to the Toronto GC in

1922. Besides, the trade commissioner forgot one important thing: He did not include greenkeepers or superintendents in his sales pitch.

## *The Depression Sets In*

As the year drew to a close the greenkeepers remembered the devastating effects of a drought followed by the heat combined with humidity which had brought summer scald and brown patch. Towards the end of the year it also became clear that the economic good times of the 1920s would not come back any time soon. The stock market crash of October 1929 had triggered a depression and, during the succeeding years, more and more greenkeepers were asked to cut costs and wages. The Toronto GC was no exception.

In January 1932, Sansom received the following letter from Fred Armitage, secretary/manager at Toronto Golf:

> *Dear Sansom:*
>
> *I am instructed by the Board of Directors to inform you, that commencing from the 16th day of January, 1932, the rate of wage to be paid English, Johnston, Nixon and Gilbert will be 40 cents per hour in place of the present 45 cents. Until further notice, all men taken on your staff who have not previously worked for the club are to receive not more than 30 cents per hour. You will therefore please make note of these important changes and inform the workmen accordingly.*
>
> *Yours faithfully,*
> *F. C. ARMITAGE*

When Sansom received this letter, he had a winter staff of four persons in addition to himself. At the height of the season, that number increased to 23. Sansom's own wages were $1,512.00 per annum or $126.00 per month. Sansom lived on the property and the house rental was valued at $300 per annum. His income therefore was the equivalent of slightly more than $150 per month.

The manner of address that Armitage used in dealing with his employee in this instance speaks of a class system that was still very much in force in Canada during the 1930s. He could have used the much more casual "Dear Bill" or perhaps even "Dear Mr. Sansom" to indicate the serious nature of the letter. Addressing someone strictly by his last name was a put down, commonly used by the higher classes in dealing with the lower classes. Greenkeeping was not a highly regarded occupation at that time, not just at Toronto GC but also at the Ladies GC in Thornhill. Superintendent Joe Blake was often called just "Blake" when the ladies wanted him to do something. Joe resented it deeply.

We can imagine how Sansom must have felt when he first received the bad tidings about the reduction of his men's wages by a nickel an hour, forty cents a day, or $ 2.00 per week. We may well wonder why Fred Armitage wouldn't just come down from his ivory tower in the clubhouse and pay a visit to the turf shop and tell the men himself. Perhaps he was just plain scared and left the onerous task to his underling.

William Sansom meanwhile knew his place in the scheme of things. The club had paid his way and his expenses to the National Greenkeepers Convention at the Pennsylvania Hotel in New York and Sansom felt obliged to thank his green committee and Mr. Armitage for enabling him to attend.

To The Greens Committee,
Toronto Golf Club, February 26th, 1932
Gentlemen:

Having had the pleasure of attending the 6th annual National Greenkeepers Golf Show and Convention held at the Hotel Pennsylvania New York City Jan. 19th-22nd, I would like to take this opportunity of thanking you and Mr. Armitage granting me the leave of absence enabling me to attend the important meeting of the Greenkeepers Association gathered together from all parts of the United States and Canada.

I attended the conferences each afternoon, the educational program being exceptionally good, papers prepared and read by experienced greenkeepers and State College Professors. Illustrated by photographs and charts shown on the screen of the various experiments carried on by the State Colleges so that we had both the practical and the scientific part making it both interesting and educational, over 600 members of the National Greenkeepers Association being present during these afternoon conferences.

I again had the honour of being re-elected to office of the Executive Board for the fourth term. There is no doubt that the annual convention and golf show is one worth while to attend. The educational program cannot be estimated too highly. Many secretary managers and greens committee as well as many others interested in turf culture attend each year. The place selected for the 1933 golf show and convention is Chicago with a recommend for Toronto in 1934.

Once more thanking you for the privilege of being able to attend the convention.

Respectfully submitted: signed: W J Sansom

*W J Sansom*

Meanwhile William Sansom was unhappy about the lowly number of Canadians that had attended the New York conference and he urged his colleagues to start planning for the next conference in Chicago. It could be that his colleagues were preoccupied with the unusually mild spring in 1932. Farmers were ploughing their fields in February and March and golfers, instead of concentrating on winter sports, were playing on the links.

H. Edgecombe, the greenkeeper at St. Andrews GC in north Toronto, reported on his experiments with dichloride of mercury, which he had applied to the greens at the rate of 4 oz. per 1000 sq. ft. with great success. Bill Pritchard at Thornhill spoke of his successes with lead arsenate applied at the rate of 5 lbs. per 1000/sq. ft. to control earthworms. His method of applying the arsenate was ingenious. He used a large drum on a wheelbarrow in the center of the green. The required amount of arsenate was placed in the drum which was filled with water and stirred thoroughly. The solution (suspension) was sprayed over the green with a homemade siphon attached to a length of hose leading from the water valve to the spraying nozzle. The operation required 20 minutes. The results were not instantaneous, but by the end of the summer the worms had vanished.

William Sansom meanwhile reflected on the disastrous summer of 1931 and made some interesting observations:

> I think we all agree that grasses are more or less dormant during the months of July and August. If this is so, we will also agree that Nature should not be interfered with too much. We should be careful and limit the use of highly soluble fertilizers during this period and that by adding an additional amount we are courting disaster.

William Sansom was about to make a radical change in his fertilizer program at the Toronto GC. Up until this point the mainstay of the program had been sulfate of ammonia. During his frequent visits to the U.S.A. and his attendance at the National Greenkeeping Conference, Sansom had come under the subtle but powerful influence of O. J. Noer, the well known agronomist with the Milwaukee Sewerage Commission.

There was no rush to make the change. In the spring of 1932, the courses in Ontario were in excellent shape without exception. Timely rains and mild weather had contributed to the continuation of these conditions. The bad memories of previous years would soon be forgotten.

Frank Hamm at the Royal York GC was excited about his experimental plots and reported that Washington and Metropolitan bents were by far the best for Canadian courses. A small quantity of Velvet bent had been slow to become established and was doing rather poorly.

The splendid summer weather continued. In August the Ontario greenkeepers paid a visit to their colleagues in western New York State and inspected plots established by the USGA Green Section. It seemed a happy summer with no serious problems, but all was not well.

The Depression was having a serious impact. The "dirty thirties" had settled in. President Sansom was not the only one who had had to cut the wages of his men. More and more greenkeepers were following suit, not just in Ontario, but in other parts of Canada as well.

G. W. Hall, greenkeeper at the 9-hole Cowansville GC in Quebec, related the following in the pages of *The National Greenkeeper*:

> To explain my problems for the year 1932, I must say
> that my Directors have been cutting expenses since the

*season began. The first thing they did was to cut my wages by 10% and they asked me to manage with one man and that I have done.*

Alfred Creed from the Winnipeg St. Charles CC reported that it had been a very trying and difficult season: "Saving here— saving there has been very hard for the greenkeeper and the last dollar has been made to count. The wages of all employees have been reduced by 10% and the workday cut back from ten to just eight hours." In spite of the cutbacks, St. Charles still employed 16 men on its green staff. Alfred Creed continues: "It looked in the spring, under the shadow of the depression, that we had a big hill to climb, but by perseverance, cooperation and strict attention to the work, we got over the hill and are just about to finish the course with a good covering of manure on the fairways and poison on the greens." Having done all he could, Alfred Creed could face the cold and long Manitoba winter with confidence. St Charles at the time consisted of 27 holes and that must have needed a lot of manure. The poison refers to dichloride of mercury, the standard treatment for snow mold control in that time.

Harold Rowswell, the greenkeeper at the Toronto Ladies GC and the brother-in-law to the club's founder Ada MacKenzie (which gave him virtual job security), was having a hard time of it during the Depression. His ancient tractor kept breaking down, but there was no money for repairs. Rowswell, who had been hired for $100.00 per month and accommodations in a house on the premises, moved to the club house with his family and without his salary. It was suggested to Rowswell that the greens be cut smaller, but he warned that the greens would be permanently reduced. Instead, the greenkeepers took a reduction in their hourly wage.

In 1936 Rowswell finally got permission to buy a new tractor which allowed him to cut the fairways twice a week instead of just once.

President Sansom summed up all he had heard about the bad times:

> *The reports that I have received from course superintend-*
> *ents all over, tell the same story, the necessity of economy*
> *this year. There have been wage reductions and there may*
> *be more.*

"Retrenchment" became the buzzword of the "dirty thirties" and it implied cutting back on expenses, reducing budgets, lowering wages, and no new machinery. William Sansom believed that many clubs would be able to retrench for a while but if the policy continued for several years, conditions on Ontario courses would eventually deteriorate.

## *Sansom the Greenkeeper: His days are numbered!*

In December of 1933, Sansom wrote to his bosses at the Toronto GC:

> *Owing to climatic conditions and other reasons such as*
> *shortage of water and lack of available plant food our fair-*
> *ways at the present time are far from being in a good*
> *healthy condition. During the period from 1916 to 1922*
> *we kept up a program of fertilizing our fairways using old*
> *stockyard manure which in those days was cheap to buy*
> *and very easy to obtain. Our fairways were in very fine*
> *condition during that period. Climatic conditions were not*
> *so severe as they have been these last few years.*

*From 1922 to 1930 we did not keep up our fertiliz-*
*ing of fairways. The old stockyard manure was no longer*
*available resulting in our fairways gradually going back*
*to the present condition.*

*The watering system we have has proven to be inade-*
*quate especially with a summer such as we have had in*
*1933. I do not believe it is possible for fairway watering*
*with anything less then 300 gallons per minute and at least*
*20 sprinklers operating. When in July the Etobicoke Creek*
*ran dry, we could barely sprinkle the greens from time to*
*time which resulted in the grasses dying out and the crab-*
*grass, chickweed, plantain and dandelions thriving.*

Sansom recommended to his Directors that they buy 35 tons
of Milorganite immediately and apply it at the rate of 1000
lbs. per acre, possibly in the spring. He also wanted to buy
ammonium sulfate and he planned to mix the Milorganite and
the sulfate as a form of weed control. After the initial application of 1000 lbs. of Milorganite in the spring, Sansom recommended an additional application of 500 lbs. per acre in the
fall. He did not believe that anything chemical could be used
satisfactorily on large areas for weed control. Some experimental work had been done at the St. Ives Research Station in
England and Sansom had written for more information. He
also reported to his directors about experiments being done at
the Cutten Club in Guelph under the directions of an OAC
professor. According to Sansom, the formulation not only
killed the chickweed but also the green. He was convinced
that with a properly balanced fertilizer program, the grass
plants would gradually spread out and crowd out the weeds.
Sansom made no suggestions what to do about the water
shortage. In subsequent communications from Armitage, we
learn that the Milorganite purchase was approved but with

more dry summers in store and insufficient water in the creek, the fairways never recovered and Sansom's days as green-keeper at the Toronto GC were numbered.

At the association level, there had been some interesting developments. Colonel Morley, longtime president and founder of the National Greenkeepers Association, had resigned in 1932 after nearly six years in office. John MacGregor of Chicago had succeeded Colonel Morley and now William Sansom was directly in line to become the third president of the NGA and the first Canadian to hold the prestigious office. The election became official at the Pittsburgh Conference. Sansom had reached the pinnacle of his profession. At 56 years of age, he had spent most of his working life at the Toronto GC, but all was not well at home.

Just months after his election to President he received the following letter from Fred Armitage:

*March 1, 1934*

*Dear Sir:*

 *Will you please keep in mind that you are not authorized to purchase goods in the name of the club—except gasoline and oil for the tractors and the dump truck—without first of all receiving official sanction.*

 *Yours truly,*
 *Secretary,*
 *F. C. ARMITAGE*

Thus put in his place, the second missive came as no surprise:

*April 9, 1934*

*Dear Sansom:*

 *Referring to our recent conversation, I now confirm the appointment, by the Directors, of Mr. George Cumming*

*to take full charge of all matters in connection with the up-*
*keep of the Grounds in order to relieve me of some of the*
*responsibilities which I have found too great during the past*
*two years owing to the ever increasing pressure of work.*

*Under this arrangement you will come into almost*
*daily contact with Mr. Cumming which should make*
*your duties a little easier, and in view of the fact that this*
*change was brought about at my request, I feel confident*
*that it should work out satisfactory to the Board of Di-*
*rectors and the Green Committee as well as to Mr. Cum-*
*ming and yourself.*

*Yours very truly,*
*Secretary,*
*F. C. ARMITAGE*

George Cumming was similarly instructed of the arrangement and further advised that: "until further notice you are not to commence teaching before the hour of 10.30 a.m. from Mondays to Fridays between April 1st and November 30th , in order that you will have the opportunity of keeping close contact with the greenkeeper for the purpose of directing his work."

Cumming was handsomely rewarded for his extra duties. During the golfing season he received an extra $150.00 per month. For the four-month winter season, the amount was reduced to $90.00 per month.

While William Sansom was acclaimed abroad as one of the top greenkeeping superintendents, at his home course he was firmly put in place under the thumb of both the golf professional and the manager. In fact, Sansom was on his way out. His days were numbered. He would enjoy one more year of glory at the helm of the National Greenkeepers Association, but his greenkeeping days at Toronto were anything but glorious.

By now, he had abdicated his responsibilities with the

Ontario Greenkeepers Association in favour of his friend and neighbour Bert Hawkins. When the 1935 conference came to Toronto, it was the crowning glory for Sansom and the high point of his career as a greenkeeper. The stately Royal York Hotel was the venue for the 9th Annual National Greenkeepers Conference for four days in February 1935.

The mayor of Toronto made the welcoming address followed by three afternoons of speeches. Among the speakers were professors from the Agriculture College in Guelph and several greenkeepers. Chester Mendenhall from Kansas City spoke about golf course maintenance, Leo Feser from Minnesota addressed preparation of putting greens for winter, and our own Bert Hawkins spoke about "Greenkeeping Yesterday and Today." One man who was destined to have the greatest impact on golf course architecture and design for the next half century gave one of his first speeches to the greenkeepers— Robert Trent Jones, who at the time was a partner in the architectural firm of Stanley Thompson.

O. J. Noer, the Milwaukee agronomist, addressed some of the major greenkeeping problems in Canada. "OJ" would be on virtually every golf course educational program from there on until his retirement 25 years later. O.J. Noer discussed many turf problems in Canada with particular emphasis on severe winter conditions in the Montreal area:

*Winter is the gravest season in Montreal. Besides more serious damage from snow mold, extensive winterkill is likely on fairways as well as greens. Fairway winterkill occurs on moist, low-lying areas, and poorly drained pockets in which water stands. In these areas bents are seldom affected, but bluegrass (Poa annua) and fescue may be completely killed. Turf recovery in the spring is necessarily slow and the establishment of new seeding uncertain, due to cool days and recurring frosts at night. Summer maintenance is relatively simple, the chief problem in the area in this district is to prevent turf loss during winter and early spring.*

In 1935 there were 586 golf clubs in Canada, divided by province as follows: Alberta 73, British Columbia 45, Manitoba 60, Saskatchewan 76, Quebec 96, Ontario 187, New Brunswick 17, Nova Scotia 23 and Prince Edward Island 9. (Newfoundland was not yet a province).

Twenty years earlier there were only 167 clubs in the Dominion. Toronto continued to lead all other cities in the number of golf clubs with 32, but Montreal ran a close second with 26. Vancouver had 10 clubs, Victoria 5, Ottawa 8, Hamilton 6 and Calgary 8. Winnipeg had more golfers per capita than any other city in North America. With a population of 217,000, it had no fewer than 17 golf courses. Edmonton is credited with having established the first municipal golf course in 1901.

In welcoming his friends and colleagues to Toronto in the winter of 1935, Sansom made some impassioned pleas.

*Let us have your constructive ideas. Try to get good members to join us and above all try to get the members back in our fold who have dropped out to no fault of their own, but rather because of the adverse times that have prevailed. You will help us to build up your organization and carry out the principles on which we are founded, namely: Justice—Benevolence and—Brotherhood.*

The Toronto conference was a great success in spite of economic times and the star of William Sansom reached its zenith. During the following months, that star would begin its downturn. The weather in 1935 was not much better than it had been the previous summer. The Etobicoke Creek ran dry again. The thousands of pounds of Milorganite did not improve the fairways at the Toronto GC and weeds were just as prevalent in 1935 as they had been before. Perhaps a hundred gallons of 2-4D could have saved Sansom's job, but that magic weed killer would not be available for at least another ten years. Sansom knew the writing was on the wall.

In 1936 the club hired a new greenkeeper, or rather a college-educated superintendent Horace Purdy. One of the members at the club, Bud McDougal (a partner of E. P. Taylor of the O'Keefe Brewing Company), had a 9-hole golf course on his estate and hired Sansom to be its caretaker. There he stayed for many more years. He occasionally attended the monthly meetings of the Ontario Greenkeepers Association. His name is mentioned in the minutes of the late 1930s and 40s. In 1973 he died in Toronto at the age of 95. Sadly, we must note that William Sansom was the first of many presidents of the American Golf Superintendents Association who would lose their jobs at the completion of their presidential terms.

Although Sansom's name is never mentioned in the 100-year history of the Toronto GC, his successor, a college-educated greenkeeper is credited with being largely responsible for turning the deplorable condition of the course around. Horace Purdy graduated from the OAC with a degree in landscaping in 1923. He was a well-known athlete at the college with prowess as a wrestler and as a rugby and hockey player. He had served for eight years as the superintendent on the course at Jasper Park Lodge in Alberta before coming to Toronto Golf in 1936. This is what Purdy said about the weeds on the golf course:

*After looking over the fairways when I first came to the Toronto Club, I wondered if by any chance that mass of buildings up in the hill could be the club house, for it seemed to me that it might well be the place for the manufacture of dandelion wine. The fairways were so badly infested that members were considering setting aside a weed fund and employing men, women or boys— whatever they could get—to do hand weeding.*

Purdy went to work and set up a series of experimental plots to test various materials. The directors bought him an expensive sprayer with a large tank and a 20-foot boom. In short order, he sprayed the fairways with sodium arsenite. One tractor was not strong enough to draw the heavy tank, so Purdy hitched up another tractor to tow in tandem with the first. While he killed some grass, it was mostly the weeds that bit the dust, not only dandelions but also chickweed and plantain. By continuing the Milorganite program that Sansom had instituted, the grasses grew in quickly where the weeds had been before. The new superintendent also improved the watering system. Because he was 'college educated,' he soon appeared at conferences as a speaker. Purdy was on the program in Detroit when the National Greenkeeping Superintendents met in 1941. He also very quickly became a member of the Ontario Greenkeepers Association, but his relationship with the local group was at times stormy. Perhaps some of the oldtimers resented him coming into the area and replacing the beloved Sansom. Whatever the reason, at various times he belonged to and then resigned from the group. When he fell behind in paying his dues, he was threatened with expulsion but cooler heads eventually prevailed. Through it all, he became known as one of the best greenkeepers in the country. When I visited Horace Purdy on his course in the summer of 1958, he was dressed in shorts and sodding the aprons around the greens with Merion Bluegrass, the new wonder turf at the time. Merion did not survive the short clipping at Toronto Golf and neither did Purdy. He was retired in the early sixties and was succeeded by Fred Charman.

## *Another Giant*

In the photo taken at the Weston GC in October of 1924, Bert Hawkins of Lakeview GC sits next to his lifelong friend and colleague, William Sansom. They remained friends and neighbors for the next 14 years until 1936, when Sansom was replaced at the Toronto GC. During that 14 years, Hawkins did not seem to mind standing in the shadow of his famous neighbor. His diligence and dedication contributed much to the survival of the Ontario Greenkeepers Association during its formative years. For the first ten years of the OGA, Hawkins served as secretary/treasurer. In 1934, when Sansom was already president of the American body, Hawkins was still listed as secretary of the Ontario Chapter. The influence of both men waned with the beginning of World War II, but they remained active and the minutes of the association indicate that both attended many of the subsequent meetings.

The Lakeview GC was considered by many to be flat and uninteresting, but the course provided an attractive view of Lake Ontario. Hawkins sought to overcome the monotony by planting trees between the fairways. In this he succeeded as many of the trees planted by Hawkins have become towering giants. The course was laid out by Hubert Strong, whose brother Leonard would become president of the GCSAA in 1953. In 1931, Lakeview hosted the Canadian Open. In preparation for that important tournament, Hawkins installed a hoseless fairway irrigation system. The par-3 17th hole was rebuilt just after the World War I and to this day is still very much as it was at the time of its creation.

Hawkins remained as president of the Ontario group until the start of World War II when John Austin of the Humber Valley GC succeeded him. In 1949, the association presented him with a scroll for his long and faithful service. (He worked at Lakeview for seven more years and died in July of 1956. His obituary in the *Toronto Star* stated that for the past three years he had been the superintendent at Lakeview. Apparently, prior to 1953 he was known as the greenkeeper. Whatever his title, he was employed by the club for more than 50 years. After his death, a framed copy of his obituary hung on a wall in the clubhouse for a long time but when his name became forgotten and his memory faded, it was passed on to this author by Murray Tucker, longtime golf professional and Canadian Golf Hall of Fame inductee. (Tucker recalled being chased off the Lakeview golf course by Hawkins when he tried to play a few holes after caddying there in the 1930s.)

Born in England, Hawkins came to Canada in 1907 with his wife Anne and daughter Lillian. A second daughter was born in Port Credit. While in England, Hawkins had been a copper and a silversmith. Upon his arrival he secured work at the Lakeview GC. He left the club for a short while but returned in 1914. In 1924, he helped form the Ontario Greenkeepers Association and in 1934 became the association's second president, a position he retained until the start of World War II.

In 1931, a New Zealand Trade Commission visited Toronto to promote the use of Chewings Fescue on Canadian golf courses. The New Zealanders advocated this fescue be used on greens as well as fairways. But they were too late. Ontario greenkeepers had already switched over to bentgrass and the golfers were happy with the new transition. Secretary

Hawkins reported: "For years fescue was the predominant grass on Canadian courses. Only in recent years have we promoted bentgrass. Fescue is fine for the fairways but I doubt if those clubs that are turning to bentgrass, will do away with it." Concluded J.H. Evans in the *Globe*: "So it seems that it will take more than a Trade Commissioner's view to cause the Canadian greenkeeper to bring his experiments with bent to an end and turn to a grass because it means trade with a sister dominion."

In February, 1935, Hawkins presented a paper at the Royal York Hotel during the National Greenkeepers of America Convention. Its title was "Greenkeeping Yesterday and Today". The early days of golf were still fresh in the mind of Hawkins and he portrayed a wonderful insight into the part played by the early greenkeepers. (See Chapter I, page 9.)

While Hawkins worked at Lakeview as the head greenkeeper during the last three years of his professional life, his title was officially changed to Golf Course Superintendent. He died at age 76 and was buried at the Springbank Cemetery. The members of the Golf Superintendents Association were pallbearers for their comrade's last journey.

# CHAPTER III

# Other Greenkeepers from Between the Wars

The first decade in the existence of the Ontario Greenkeepers Association was dominated by William Sansom and Bert Hawkins. There were, however, several other well known greenkeepers in the industry who had an impact on course conditioning during the 1930s. Foremost among them in the Toronto area was William Chinery.

## William D. Chinery, Greenkeeper
## York Downs Golf Club (1924–1935)

William Chinery was born in England about 1875. He was trained as a professional gardener specializing in sports turf on pleasure grounds. During his training, he gained much practical experience in the maintenance of cricket pitches, tennis and croquet courts, as well as estate lawns. When he arrived in Canada in 1913 just prior to the first World War,

W.D. *Chinery of Eglinton, Canada who* speaks on club house gardening. *Photo provided by GCSAA.*

he naturally endeavored to follow his profession but found that there was little scope for "that class of gardening in Canada at that time." Good fortune put him in touch with George Cumming, the pro/greenkeeper at the Toronto GC. Mr. Cumming encouraged him to take up golf course work. Just a few years later he was put in charge of the Scarborough GC and he remained there for five years.

Opportunity knocked again when York Downs was constructed in the early 1920s. Mr. Chinery landed the job as head greenkeeper and quickly established himself as an expert on greenkeeping in the Toronto area. He wrote several articles for the *National Greenkeeper* magazine, a publication of the newly formed National Greenkeepers Association (1926). His writing was forthright and provocative and he challenged his readers to disagree with his opinions. He also gained credibility when he spoke at the early conferences of the fledgling American association.

On harrows, Mr. Chinery opines that he considered them one of "the best implements that any golf club can buy." He claims they are invaluable for pulverizing topdressing, for working up the roughs, and for removing worm casts on the

*The quaint old greenkeepers cottage on the property of the York Downs Golf and Country Club.*

fairways. We must assume that Chinery was referring to chain harrows which, when dragged with the teeth in the upward position do a fine job of smoothing the surface. With the teeth downward, chain harrows scratch the turf and thin the thatch. It is a known method still in use to this day.

The soil of the valley holes at York Downs was a "friable black loam inclining to sand." On the upper holes, the soil was a very "adhesive clay given to baking and cracking." This deplorable condition called for action and Chinery and spent his first winters applying sand with good results. He used more then 5000 loads! In addition, he topdressed the approaches with compost.

At a time when many courses still had fescue greens, York Downs decided to follow the modern trend and seeded their greens with South German Bentgrass. Some thought that the new bent greens required very little topdressing and that the bent would choke out the weeds. "All bunkum" stated Chinery emphatically, who was a firm believer in timely top-dressings but not before the greens were first weeded with sharp toothed rakes! The rakes brought up the runners and made the weeds stand up. It took 2–3 yards of finely screened compost placed in heaps in the proximity of the green. Since York Downs did not possess a topdressing machine, the work was done by strong men with square mouthed shovels and bamboo poles to rub the topdressing into the turf. "The poles should not be too whippy," Mr. Chinery warned, or else they would lack strength to work the soil into the turf. Six men could topdress a green in about an hour.

Chinery's problems at York Downs were not limited to clay soils and topdressing. On an early September morning in 1925, a crew member informed him that the seventh green had been torn up by crows. A skeptical Chinery assumed the information was an exaggeration but went out to check anyway. To his consternation, he found that the green had indeed been damaged and it appeared as if "a litter of pigs had been having a rooting party." Now follows a tale reminiscent of the movie *Caddie Shack* 70 years later. Chinery realized he had a serious problem: not one green but several had been uprooted by varmints in search of the juicy white grubs of the June beetle. Quick action was required. A sleuth by nature, Chinery concluded from the tracks in the dew that he was dealing with skunks and not crows. He devised an ingenious method to get rid of the skunks once and for all. From the clubhouse kitchen he obtained some lard and fashioned look-alike "grubs" which he doused with strychnine and planted in the greens. It worked! Over the next week he killed 17 skunks! Chinery observed: "With their ranks decimated, we had a little respite though there were one or two that still persisted." Evidently, they had become wise to the fake grubs. Chinery now played his trump card: On a moonlit night he stole from the barn, armed with two guns! Hidden by the trees in the rough, he carefully checked around the course and found his enemy at work on the approach to a green. Aware of "Mr. Skunk's reputation," he circled his enemy respectfully. Being a good sport and not wanting to shoot a sitting duck, he shouted and whistled to no avail as the "beasty" kept on feeding. He loaded his guns with shells and from 40 feet away, he blasted away. The end was anticlimactic: the dead skunk's skin became a memento in the York Downs barn and Chinery was "pleased to report that we have not suffered again by their depredations." The Society for the Prevention of Cruelty to Animals might not have approved, but it happened long before they became active.

In 1927, Brown Patch Disease was already a problem on the greens at York Downs. Chinery closely watched the action of bichloride of mercury as a means of control and was anxious to compare notes with his confreres who had already experienced the disease. As for assistant greenkeepers, Chinery trained two young men; one took over the 27-hole Thornhill GC and another went to Beachgrove near Windsor. (He did not mention their names.)

In the spring of 1929 Chinery once again took pen in hand. This time the subject was lime. One would not think that a golf course with a pH of well over seven (and in some parts higher than eight) would be in need of lime, but Chinery sees some benefit for the heavy soils at York Downs: "I am convinced," he wrote, "after years of practical experience and observation that lime applied to heavy soils does vastly more good than harm!" "Lime promotes deeper root action," he continued, adding that "lime has proved to be a great aid against certain fungoid pests." Not once in this dissertation on lime did Chinery mention the pH scale.

Just one year later, in the April 1930 issue of the *National Greenkeeper*, he pontificated about "High Speed Greenkeeping" in a seven page article. In all likelihood, the article was a reprint of a talk presented at the Louisville Conference in early 1930. Two things were foremost on Chinery's mind: bentgrass and Brown Patch Disease (BPD). The introduction of bentgrass on putting greens had made its appearance barely a dozen years previous and greenkeepers were just learning to live with this new grass. Many applied copious amounts of ammonium sulfate, as much as four to six lbs. of material per 1000 sq. ft. once and even twice per month. The lush growth often led to outbreaks of Brown Patch Disease. Here was Chinery at his best:

> *When one enumerates the long list of fertilizers, both chemical and organic that are placed on the market to produce two blades of grass where only one grew before, one may ask this question: Are we not using too much dope?*

Chinery certainly thought so!

> *In the old days it was considered good judgment to avoid the use of any fertilizer that was of a hastening or burning nature. One cannot outrage nature for long without suffering the consequences. We have been led by the ear by some experts with their theoretical bunkum so that years of practical experience have been thrown in the discard.*

Chinery began to suspect that there was a relationship between extreme acidity and Brown Patch Disease or: "Should I use the term algae?" He seemed unsure about the nature of the different diseases. He continued: "I may say that the large, irregular Brown Patch has been more prevalent than the round or Dollar Brown Patch although the latter has proved more deadly." Therein lies a dire warning for the future; the dreaded Dollar Spot Disease was about to gain foothold on Ontario greens but the most troublesome Brown Patch continued to be Algae. According to Chinery, when greens are situated in the open on high sandy ground with good drainage, one need not worry about Algae, but when drainage is poor in low shady locations, look out! Rather than curing the Algae, he believed it was wiser to change the growing conditions. Chinery continued to use lime, especially on the crusty clay soils of the upper holes at York Downs. He had also learned that bentgrass grows equally well on sour and sweet soils and he also discovered that lead arsenate was "effectual in the control of certain weeds and is a perfectly safe worm exterminator." The environmentalist in Chinery advised that it "is not wise to be too drastic in one's efforts to get rid of all the worms."

At that time, J. H. Evans was the golf editor for the *Toronto Globe* (later *Globe and Mail*) who often commented on the work of "greenkeepers and superintendents." He mostly quoted the words and wisdom of William Sansom. Often, he referred to Joseph Stanfield, the greenkeeper at Mississaugua, and on occasion, Bert Hawkins at Lakeview and Howard Lloyd at Rosedale. Not once in all his writing on golf for the *Toronto Globe* (which is reprinted in the *National Greenkeeper*) did Evans mention Chinery. Yet Chinery was by far the best writer of all his contemporaries.

In the summer of 1930, the executive committee of the National Greenkeepers Association met for a few days in Toronto. They were guests of William Sansom, now vice president of the group. These gentlemen travelled in style and stayed at the Royal York Hotel, probably courtesy of the association, since a few years later, the National held its first annual conference and exhibits in Canada at the very same hotel (1935). Between meetings they toured nine area golf courses but, again, York Downs was not included. The question bears asking: Was the outspoken Mr. Chinery being shunned by his colleagues? At the conclusion of the visit the Americans were feted at the Old Mill Restaurant on the banks of the Humber. There were 31 guests at the dinner, most of them greenkeepers, but William D. Chinery was not among them!

In 1933, William Chinery once more made headlines in the *National Greenkeeper Reporter* when he recounted his experiences with grubs and skunks. From then on, there was total silence. In the minute book of the Ontario Greenkeepers Association dated January 12, 1937, it appears that a special written invitation was extended to Mr. Chinery and Mr. Purdy to invite them to the annual luncheon at the Royal York Hotel, but there is no record to indicate that Chinery showed up for the luncheon.

Chinery had two sons. One of the boys won the caddy tournament at York Downs and later both worked in the pro shop at York Downs under Willie Freeman. They became head pros in their own right, one at Burlington and the other at Dundas Valley. Bill Jr. was shown on the CPGA executive committee in 1950. Norman Smith, longtime golf professional at York Downs, knew the sons and recalled hearing of Chinery, Sr. but he never met him personally. Smith respectfully referred to Chinery as Mr. Chinery, an indication of the respect the old time greenkeeper had earned at York Downs. Chinery was succeeded by Jack Widgett who lasted only a few years. Norm MacDonald took over in 1945 and stayed with the club until the course was sold and the club moved to Unionville.

MacDonald lived on the old course in a boarded-over log house with a wishing well in the front yard. By the time this author became acquainted with him, MacDonald was married to the club's bookkeeper, who was his third wife; the first two wives died with the passing of time. MacDonald was at least a generation older than the bookkeeper he had married. When the old greenkeeper turned 70 and was still actively working at York Downs, his colleagues organized a birthday party. Among the many gifts received was a dozen condoms, which caused much hilarity among his assembled friends.

MacDonald kept a finely manicured golf course that was the pride of the membership. He stayed on the job well into his 70th year and was loved and respected by the members. When the club moved to Unionville, they hired Kimmo Salonen, a Finlander with a degree from Penn State University. MacDonald died shortly thereafter and was carried to his grave by his fellow superintendents.

When Chinery finished his days at York Downs, he freelanced for a while. Keith Nisbet recalled meeting Chinery at the Box Grove GC near Markham. Chinery worked with Jimmy Johnson, golf professional at Rosedale who was also an occasional golf course architect, Box Grove being one of Johnson's best known projects. Nisbet's visit to Box Grove took place in the early 1950s and he recalled Chinery as a man of small stature who vociferously advocated the benefits of native bentgrass. That's in line with Chinery's greenkeeping philosophy from his York Downs days. Box Grove was known as the private reserve of Nelson Davis, a car dealer in north Toronto. The course was reputed to be one of the best conditioned layouts in the Toronto area. Perhaps Chinery could take some of the credit for that. Box Grove later was bought by the IBM Company for the use of its staff.

# John Anderson at the Cedarbrook GC, Scarborough

This course was established in 1923 and may have been laid out by Captain Perkins, the pro at the Brantford GC. Encompassing 159 acres in total, 100 acres were ploughed and seeded with a mixture of 20% Chewings Fescue, 40% Kentucky bluegrass and 40% Red Top at 250 lbs. per acre. The greens at first were "of a temporary nature," according to John Anderson, the greenkeeper. Nine greens were then rebuilt and planted with bentgrass stolons. The stolonized bent must have seemed like a 'wondergrass' to Anderson because he wrote: "The qualities of the bentgrass greens are as follows: Even texture, smoother putting surface, resistance to winter kill, less liable to diseases, eliminates weeds and weeding by producing a heavy covering of uniform colour." To feed the greens, Anderson used light and frequent applications of sulphate of ammonia every two weeks and topdressed with a sandy loam regularly. Anderson had a nursery on the property of Washington Bentgrass (from the Dr. Piper visit, via the Toronto GC) from which he obtained the stolons to plant the new greens. He also purchased bentgrass seed that must have been Colonial Bentgrass seed, perhaps Island Bent from Prince Edward Island. He also tried to harvest the seed from his bentgrass nursery but we never do learn how that experiment turned out. It probably did not work, because special equipment is required to harvest the very fine bentgrass seed.

Anderson was all too well aware that one cannot grow grass without water and he had an underground system of pipes to water the tees and greens. A 7hp Century electric motor drove a pump near the Highland Creek. A system of 2″ pipes, gradually reducing to ½ inch at the end of lines, provided sufficient water to keep the grass on the tees and greens alive. The fairways depended solely on rainwater for survival.

## Green Staff

Four men attended to the 18 greens which were cut by hand machines (No motor!). They also attended to the weeding, fertilizing, and topdressing. One man looked after the tees, moving the markers each morning, and did scything when necessary. Another person with a Staude tractor pulling a 5-gang Shawnee mower cut the fairways. The roughs were done with a "one horse hay mower." We must assume that a hay mower is just like a side-mounted sickle bar mower.

Anderson also used an additional Staude tractor as a power plant to drive the compost machines and to screen the material for topdressing, "a good supply of which is kept on hand because bentgrass greens require more frequent topdressing than ordinary greens."

A photo of John Anderson and the club's secretary, Mr. M. A. Chadwick accompanies his article. Anderson looks as if he had just finished topdressing. Chadwick wears a tie. The men are seated in upright chairs in front of the club house. In a postscript, Anderson confesses that Chadwick helped him write the article.

The 1931 Directory of Golf Clubs of the Empire still listed J. Anderson as the greenkeeper at Cedar Brook, but Mr. Chadwick had been replaced. In September 1947, John Anderson was made an honorary member of the Ontario Greenkeepers Association.

# Fred Hamm,
# Greenkeeper, Royal York GC

Fred Hamm, the first greenkeeper at the Royal York GC, was a greenkeeper of several courses in the state of Florida prior to his arrival in Toronto, where he won much acclaim with his experimental work on grasses. The plots at the Royal York GC were frequently visited by the area greenkeepers. Hamm must have returned to the United States, because there is no record of him in subsequent directories.

# Howard Lloyd,
# Greenkeeper, Rosedale GC

Howard Lloyd worked with architect Donald Ross to build the new and existing Rosedale GC. As was customary, the American architect spent very little time on the job and Howard Lloyd did most of the work but received very little credit. At Rosedale, the name of the architect is still remembered but the efforts of the hardworking greenkeeper have long been forgotten. Howard Lloyd was a close friend of William Sansom and he was popular with all his colleagues. Because of his mature age and his happy visage, he was often referred to as "Smiling Dad." In 1935, he became ill and was granted a year's leave of absence, which he spent on a farm near Grimsby, Ontario. His colleagues visited him regularly at the farm, but Smiling Dad never recovered and died a few years later.

## Charlie Robinson,
## Greenkeeper, Thistletown GC

Charlie Robinson was one of the original members of the Ontario Greenkeepers Association. Bruce Summers worked with Robinson and learned greenkeeping tricks from the old timer. Summers recalled that Charlie Robinson would take off every Tuesday to Webb Seed to visit Blondie Wilson who at the time was the agronomic expert. Robinson did not drive a car and had to depend on public transportation as a means of conveyance.

## George Hunter,
## Greenkeeper, Brantford GC

George Hunter, a longtime greenkeeper at Brantford GC, is mentioned in the 1937 minutes of the Ontario Greenkeepers Association. He hosted several meetings for the Toronto group and was proud to demonstrate the hoseless watering system on the Brantford Course to his colleagues. The system had been installed under the direction of Bill Powel, a professional engineer and a club member at Brantford. Powel remained green chairman for 29 years and during that time he helped many other golf courses with their watering systems. Hunter was also an active member of the Western Ontario Greenkeepers Association.

## Jack Stanfield
## Greenkeeper, Mississaugua GC

Jack Stanfield hosted several meetings of the association at his club and also prepared his course for the Canadian Open.

# Jim Hickman, Greenkeeper, London Highland GC (1915?–1958)

Jim Hickman was a charter member of the Ontario association and is listed as Vice-President at one time, but he found the travelling to the Toronto area bothersome since he did not drive a car. In 1929, he started the Western Ontario Greenkeepers Association and dominated that group for many years.

# Bill Pritchard, Greenkeeper, Thornhill GC

Pritchard started at Thornhill in 1927 when the club was in its infancy. He became well known in the industry and in 1937 he made headlines in the *Toronto Star* with his methods of stolonizing greens. After the war, he moved to the Royal Ottawa GC where he continued his experimental work on an extensive nursery on that course.

# Harold Rowswell, Greenkeeper, Toronto Ladies GC

Harold Rowswell was the first greenkeeper at the Toronto Ladies GC and an active participant during the early days of the Ontario Greenkeepers Association.

# Jack Abbott, Greenkeeper, Islington Golf Course

Jack Abbott, at one time farmed what is now the Islington GC. His family sold the farm to the Islington members and Jack was part of the package. He remained greenkeeper at Islington for many years, and it was said that Jack Abbott held a mortgage on the property, which gave him some job security. In 1938 he became greenkeeper at the Rosedale GC. He served as president of the OGA and also as a director of the American association. Abbot confided to this author many years ago that he felt he had no influence on the Board of Directors of the American association and he served for only one two-year term.

# Kirby,
# Greenkeeper, Lambton GC

Kirby was quite active in the Greenkeepers association but he was often at odds with his colleagues and sometimes he refused to pay his dues. The executive struggled over what to do with Kirby. The members recognized his contributions and since he was one of the founding fathers, they did not really want to kick Kirby out. They reached a happy compromise. Since Kirby was near retirement at his club, he was given an honorary membership. The next year he was succeeded at Lambton by Dick Homewood (1940).

# Bill Bluett, Greenkeeper,
# Glen Mawr GC, Don Mills 1935

Bill Bluett had his start at this Stanley Thompson-designed golf course that has since been subdivided. All that remains today is the old club house which now serves as a community center. Bluett later replaced Jack Stanfield at Mississaugua from where he graduated several young men as future superintendents. Bluett was a strong supporter of the greenkeeping movement from its very early days and in later life became president of the group. Among the men that Bluett graduated from Mississaugua were Phil Glover, Dick Homewood, and Art Dodson.

When Bluett reached retirement age, the Mississaugua GC at various times hired assistants to take the place of the old greenkeeper. This author was interviewed by the green chairman at the Toronto GC in 1958 (the Toronto GC at the time was a private men's club) and offered the position. After the interview, it seemed prudent to stop at the greens barn and discuss the appointment with Bluett, who was not impressed. In fact, he sent me packing in no uncertain terms and I never dared report for work.

## *Louis Cole, Greenkeeper, Burlington GC*

Louis Cole was the first greenkeeper at the Burlington GC where he started his career in 1922. He stayed at the club until his retirement 50 years later in 1972. Although he was not professionally active in either the Western or the Ontario associations, he was a strong supporter of both groups and attended meetings regularly. Louis Cole also belonged to the American association. He was a congenial man who had many friends in the industry and among the members at the Burlington GC. When he retired, he was succeeded by his son Ray which seems to have led to conflict among the greens staff. A labour union tried to organize the golf course workers. The club countered the move by outsourcing the maintenance of the golf course to a contractor. Ray Cole then moved to the Royal Ottawa GC.

# The Early Presidents of the Ontario Greenkeepers Association

1924–1932  Wm. Sansom
1933–1941  Bert Hawkins

# The Western Ontario Greenkeepers Association

In southwestern Ontario, greensmen under the leadership of Jim Hickman, greenkeeper at the London Highland, formed an association in 1929, known variously as the Western Ontario Greensmen Association, later as the Western Ontario Greenkeepers Association, and later still as the Western Ontario Golf Superintendents Association (WOGSA). Hickman is generally acknowledged as the founder of the group, but it is suspected that he had much help from Fred Grightmire, the greenkeeper at Dundas Valley GC. Another early supporter was George Hunter, the greenkeeper at the Brantford GC. Grightmire did not start working at the Dundas Valley Club until 1931, so we must assume that Hickman was very much on his own in the beginning, and it was not until later when the association had become established that he received much needed help from other greenkeepers in southwestern Ontario.

Hickman was an English gardener who had immigrated to Canada in the early part of the century. His first golf position was with the Beaconsfield GC near Montreal. In the midtwenties he became greenkeeper at the Highland GC. The story of "The Western" for its first 25 years is, in effect, very much the story of Jim Hickman.

Hickman was the quintessential English gardener who

took great pride in his flowers. Every spring he would cut pea brush and dead twigs to which he would string sweet-peas. He also grew prizewinning tomatoes which he exhibited at the Western Fall Fair in London. The expectations of the Highland golfers were modest in the years before the war and Hickman had no trouble meeting them. After all, he knew how to grow things and grass was no exception. He took great pride in the stolon nursery on his course. His greenkeeping knowledge was mostly learned from contact with other greenkeepers in the area. Hickman never had a driver's license and when he attended the meetings of his association he often took the train. On the golf course he used an old bicycle to get around, no mean feat, since Highland GC is by no means a flat layout. Later he learned to drive a jeep on the golf course, but he never took the jeep on the road since he was not licensed.

As Hickman grew older, he experienced the common peril of young, low handicap golfers making unreasonable demands that he could not meet within his limited budget. The last few years of his greenkeeping life were not the happiest ones; in fact, they were quite miserable years, caused by the harassment he received from a small number of malcontents. In 1956, his earnings were $3100 per year. By the time he retired the amount had been raised to $3600 which is $75.00 per week. Highland GC paid him a pension of $100 per month. Hickman was succeeded by a college-educated superintendent who knew absolutely nothing about greenkeeping but impressed the Highland directors with his brilliance. The college graduate was paid $100 per week. (That college graduate is the author of this book.) Much the same had happened at Toronto Golf when Purdy succeeded Sansom and it would be repeated time and again as the profession of greenkeeping advanced over the years.

During the first years of the western association many of the meetings were held either at Dundas Valley or at the Highland Golf Clubs. Hickman had a strong sense of social justice and right from the beginning his group included not just greenkeepers but all greensmen employed on golf courses. At one time he tried to convince his colleagues that all members should be issued a membership card and that without such a card they would not be able to find employment at member clubs. The members of the Western smelled a rat and turned down Hickman's proposal to unionize the golf course workers industry.

Hickman also loved to have fun with his fellow greensmen. He was a respectable player, often breaking 100, and he encouraged all his colleagues to play the game. On Sunday September 23, 1934, the group organized its first golf tournament at Highland GC. The entry fee was 50 cents and 25 greenkeepers and greensmen teed off. At the end of the competition, there was a tie for first between Ernie Owen and H. Shepherd of Thames Valley. Both scored 86, but Owen won in the play-off and received "The Hickman Cup." Ernie Owen was listed as being from Highland GC. Later, he worked at London Hunt and eventually he became the greenkeeper at Sarnia GC. Also in attendance at this first tournament were greenkeepers Arthur Nixey from the London Hunt and George Hunter from Brantford GC. Both were staunch supporters of the fledgling association.

In 1935, both the annual meeting and the golf tournament were held at the Union GC in St. Thomas. Hickman who had had enough of being president, nominated the host greenkeeper D. Williams as the new leader of the group. Such informal elections have been the earmark of the Western group ever since.

In 1934, the dues were raised to $2.00 for greenkeepers

and $1.00 for greensmen, but that proved to be a poor decision since the association rapidly lost members in the depression years and the motion to raise the dues was rescinded. Williams proved to be a poor administrator as no records were kept for the next five years. We really don't know what happened to Williams, but by 1941, Fred Grightmire had become president and in spite of the war, the association moved back on track. Golf competitions continued, but no winners are recorded. The tournament was played at Highland in 1938 and at Westmount in 1939. The host greenkeeper at Westmount, Howard Snider, began to take an active part in the association. In 1940, the tournament once again moved to Dundas Valley GC.

In 1942, there were 46 members who paid $1.00 each to belong to the association. Even during the war, there were no interruptions in the regular meetings. In 1946, the dues were raised to $2.00. Elwood McArthur of the Glendale GC took the helm at the urging of his dear friend Jim Hickman. Elwood served as president during 1949 and 1950 and was followed by Ed Walls, greenkeeper at the Hamilton GC. Walls had been assistant to John Sutherland, one of the first bonafide greenkeepers in Ontario, who had retired in 1937.

In 1955, the association celebrated its 25th anniversary. This date is somewhat peculiar, since the Western was supposed to have been founded in 1929. The arithmetic just does not add up. Maybe the blame and the confusion can be placed at the feet of Morley Findlay, the greenkeeper at Brantford GC who had taken over from George Hunter. Findlay was a sportsman, a hockey player in his younger days, and a keen golfer with a 6 handicap. He won many golfing competitions including several McClumpha Tournaments. Findlay was most reluctant to become president in 1953. He turned down one of the few aboveboard elections in the Western's history and Hickman once more filled the gap. The following year Findlay gave in, but by that time they were a year behind and the quarter century celebrations were held in 1955 (where else but at the Highland GC). The greensmen once again competed for the Hickman Cup, but the winner is not recorded.

Findlay had enough of being president and this time was bailed out by Fred Grightmire who recognized the need to keep the Western moving. Findlay moved to Maple City GC, where he had an unfortunate accident: while watching his men trim rough with rotary mowers, one of the cutters fired out a golf ball which fractured Findlay's leg in three different places. He was not on crutches for long. Ironically, the operator of the rotary mower ended up marrying Findlay's daughter, Lorraine. Findlay's golfing exploits continued and his greenkeeping skills were good enough to land one of the top jobs in the province; the new London Hunt designed by Robert Trent Jones. He stayed there until his retirement.

Meanwhile the western association continued to prosper. Fred Grightmire persuaded one more old-timer to take the reigns: Howard Snider from Westmount was placed in charge of the association in 1957 and 1958. Fred Grightmire's son John had become golf course superintendent at the Beverley GC near Hamilton and was quickly induced into the presidency following Snider. He served for four years from 1959–1962 and was succeeded by Bill Robertson from the Port Colborne GC. Robertson was as popular with Western members as he was with the members of his club on the shores of Lake Ontario. The Port Colborne golfers honoured Bill with an evening of appreciation and a new set of golf clubs for 25 years of service.

Snyder at Westmount had retired and was succeeded by Herb Creed, one of a long line of Creeds from western Canada. Herb Creed was a founding member of the Canadian

Golf Superintendents Association in 1965 and that same year he became president of the western group. He is remembered mainly for being stuck with a liquor bill when his colleagues drank to excess while attending a meeting at Westmount. For the record, the association reimbursed Herb Creed for his largesse.

At various times during its existence, the Western was threatened with being swallowed by the older and more sophisticated Ontario Golf Superintendents Association. It never came to pass. The Western's strength has always been its strong sense of camaraderie and the informal and congenial ways in which its meetings have been conducted. Since its beginning, Western meetings have featured a free and open exchange of information, so that everyone who attends learns something. Founder Jim Hickman was a fun man with a ready smile and his successors have perpetuated that image. In fact, the Western has always attracted superintendents from the Toronto area to its meetings. William Chinery of York Downs attended the Western meetings in 1946 and 1947 before retiring to the IBM club and the Moote brothers from Toronto were avid participants in Western affairs. The leadership of Western has always been hospitable and friendly which guarantees good turnouts at the meetings. Under the leadership of Nicol Thompson and John Piccolo from Niagara, the association seems to have moved away from the London and Kitchener area. Steve Miller and Bob Kennedy, respectively from Burlington GC and Niagara Parks, continued that trend, but under John Taylor the association has occasionally ventured back into western Ontario with meetings in Guelph, Woodstock, and Kitchener. While other associations have suffered from dwindling participation, the Western is still very much a strong association with well attended meetings.

## *Historical Events*

1920 Stanley Thompson began his remarkable career as a golf course architect.

1922 The club managers became organized

1923 Horace Purdy graduated from the OAC and became the first college-educated superintendent in Canada when he accepted a job at the Jasper Park GC.

1924 The Ontario Greenkeepers Association is founded at the Weston GC on Oct. 4.

1925 Steel shafts begin to replace hickory-shafted clubs.

1926 Five hundred golf courses dot the map of Canada.

1928 Ontario greenkeepers organized their first equipment show at the Rosedale.

1930 Second equipment show held at the Royal York GC.

---

THE TORONTO DAILY STAR, Saturday, May 22, 1937

---

# BACKSTAGE AT THORNHILL

*Greenskeeper's Life Highly Interesting—*
*Creeping Bent Nurseries Maintained—Seeded Greens*
*Give Way to Sodded Surfaces*

By Fred Jackson

One of the most interesting chores in this daily life of sports reporting is an assignment to go back-stage in the sportive whirl and see just what makes the wheels go round.

Back of all the glamorous highlights of sport there is always the setting . . . the work to be done before the highly publicized performers plunge into the heart of competition.

What does the average golfer know about back-stage life around a golf course?

How do the clubs get such richly verdant greens? . . . smooth as the finest carpet . . . evenly textured . . . sound surfaces despite constant

*103*

watering . . . healthy despite continual feeding . . . true at times as even a billiard table.

## Greens Are Sodded

With all this in mind we moved along to the Thornhill club, where greenkeeping and all that goes with it is well organized and a fair example of what goes on in the leading clubs of this district.

Time was when most golf greens were seeded propositions. Now most of that business is over and in the big clubs when a new green is required the head greenkeeper simply sends his men over to the creeping bent nursery and they cut yards and yards of beautifully kept sod to be transported over to the new putting surface.

The story of this sod is rather intriguing.

At Thornhill an extensive nursery is maintained.

## Use Washington Bent

Over in one spot you will see the Washington creeping bent stolon beds where this most valuable grass is maintained in its initial stages. When we visited Thornhill men were busy digging stolons and tossing them into a dump truck to be carted to a new nursery being created. Peek at the LOWER RIGHT picture in the above layout and you can see the stolon beds and the stolons which look to the ordinary layman as heavily-grassed sods.

In the LOWER LEFT picture you can see men feeding a machine which cuts the stolons into fine pieces. This mixture is then tossed over some prepared and fertilized ground and then top-dressed. Over-head is a watering-system and with judicious watering and careful weeding thousands of square feet of beautiful grass is produced, an example of which is demonstrated by Bill Pritchard. Head greenkeeper in the UPPER RIGHT corner of the layout.

## Stands the Gaff

It has been found by most clubs that Washington creeping bent stands the gaff of Canadian winters better than other varieties of grass. It is a peculiar grass which spreads all over the thickens quickly. In time if left alone it becomes so matted and thick that air cannot penetrate to the roots. Thus frequently it has to be top-dressed—spiked and thinned out.

This modern development in golf greens is so much superior to the old way of seeding a green that there is really no comparison. Of course the bent comes from seed but it is extremely rare and most clubs purchase stolons and thus start their own beds. At Thornhill a new thirteenth green was put down last fall with over 6,000 square feet of turf. Right now it is in fine condition and being used every day. Such time saving could not have been possible under the old conditions.

But the mere item of grass is not all that makes the golfing wheel spin.

Remember the heat wave last summer when lawns were ruined and the rain just wouldn't come down?

## Continual Watering

That was a trying time for the golf clubs with their vast acreage of grass to be maintained.

From the first of May to the end of August last year two men worked all night from 5:30 p.m. to 7:30 a.m. watering all fairways and greens. At a pumping capacity of 300 gallons a minute you figure out many thousands of gallons of water were pumped out in one night. Then if you want a real headache multiply that by as many weeks and months between May and August.

Fairway watering is a big thing in golf course upkeep. Thornhill maintains an eighteen-hole course and a smaller nine-hole course. Every fairway of the 27 is piped down the centre with numerous outlets, thus enabling the head greenkeeper to toss plenty of water on the course when the weatherman turns contrary.

Luckily at Thornhill the "Little Don" winds through the property, thus ensuring an ample supply of water without having to depend and pay for township supply.

Space will not permit too much enlargement on the theme.

But here is a line-up of some equipment necessary to keep a golf course going.

Two tractors with seven and five-mower units for fairways.

One truck and two dumping bodies.

Twenty-four hand mowers, which cost around $85 each. One power mower.

One compost mixer . . . one plow . . . one disc harrow . . . two chain harrows . . . one tractor spike disc machine . . . one Holden spreader for spreading fertilizer . . . fourteen wheelbarrows . . . a completely fitted machine-shop . . . a forge . . . 3,000 feet of hose . . . 29 various types of sprinklers for tees and greens . . . 22 large travelling sprinklers for the fairways and dozens of other smaller items.

That sounds like big business.

It is!

"Reprinted with permission from *The Toronto Star Syndicate*"

*Above: Workers Sprigging a Green. Right: Bill Pritchard, Greenkeeper, Thornhill Golf Club. Below: Backstage at Thornhill. Reprinted from* Toronto Daily Star *May 22, 1937*

# CHAPTER IV

# John Gray,
# Greenkeeper, Essex GC

*"A gentle and loveable man"*

1885–1958

Whil e most of the early greenkeeping activity was taking place in Central Ontario in the region that has become known as "The Golden Horseshoe," the rest of the province was by no means without its stars in the profession. At the St. Catharine's GC, Tom Styles was highly regarded for his talent, as was Nixon at the London Hunt Club. Somewhat isolated from the rest of the province was John Gray, longtime green-keeper at the Essex GC near Windsor. Gray had arrived in Windsor in the early part of the century from Scotland. He promptly became involved in building the first Essex golf course and stayed on as the club's first greenkeeper.

Being a native Scotsman with a strong sense of civic duty,

*John Gray*

Gray quickly joined the war effort when World War I broke out. Before he went overseas, he married his sweetheart Evelyn Jane Reid, who lived across the street from the golf course. Upon his return it did not take long for Gray to become once more involved with golf. He built a course near Chicago for Harry Colt, then another for Donald Ross in Detroit. When Essex had to move further out of town, John Gray was called upon to build the new course.

Donald Ross was the architect of choice, but Ross was busy building Pinehurst #2 and the Seminole GC in Florida. Ross came to Essex only for a few days to do a routing plan and prepare sketches of the greens. He left behind a surveyor to stake the greens, but the work to build the golf course was left in the capable hands of John Gray who was after all, quite experienced in the construction of golf courses. With great enthusiasm Gray tackled the task and quickly got caught up in the spirit of the new project. He cut down trees and removed the stumps with dynamite. He used horses with buckets and scrapers and dozens of men to move dirt from one place to another to elevate the greens and tees on the flat Essex landscape. He made sure the greens had plenty of surface drainage but he was also one of the first to install french drains off the greens where water might collect. In some cases, he modified the Donald Ross design for easier maintenance (such as the #5 green).

Gray did not limit his activities to the building of golf

courses. From the beginning he was involved in the superintendent's movement. Although he was not present at the original meeting at the Sylvania CC in Toledo, Ohio, he did attend the first winter conference of the National Greenkeepers Association the following year in 1927 in Chicago. A photograph of the lecture hall shows Gray in the second row, larger than life. John Gray became the only Canadian charter member of the new association and thereafter he attended the national meetings regularly. When William Sansom retired as past president in February 1935, John Gray was immediately elected or appointed as a director. Thus the Canadian influence on the American association continued unabated.

Not only was John Gray active at the national level, he was also involved in the Michigan Border Cities Golf Course Superintendents Association. The Essex GC often hosted meetings of that group and John Gray also volunteered his help in the chapter's affairs. In 1937 he became president of the Michigan Border Cities Association.

Gray's involvement with the Michigan chapter broadened his horizon to include the Michigan State College Turf Department in East Lansing. It was particularly Dr. Tyson's work in soils that interested Gray. Soon John Gray became a self-taught agronomist, who without the benefit of formal schooling, made a name for himself and became a recognized authority in southwestern Ontario not only on golf course maintenance but also in landscaping. For a while he served as Trustee on the MSU advisory board.

The highlight of John Gray's career came in 1940 just as another war was brewing. The occasion was the annual meeting of the National Greenkeeping Association at the Hotel New Yorker in New York City. John Gray became the ninth president and the second Canadian to take the helm of his professional association. This is what John Gray had to say:

*The pages of history turn. A beloved and capable leader has entrusted the gavel to my hands. It is my sincere hope that I can approach the task, which confronts me with the same measure of success as my predecessor. I appreciate the vote of confidence and trust that it will not be misplaced.*

Then Gray reflected on the conference that had just been:

*Days crowded with work and play, hours filled with planning, guarding old friendships and reaching for new handclasps, and picking up morsels of education and inspiration. All of these can be regarded as typical of what we wish for the future of the GSA(Greenkeeping Superintendents Association). It has been said that nothing grows without nourishment. We, men of the soil are well aware of that truth.*

War clouds were gathering and in his next message to the readers of the *Greenkeeper's Reporter*, John Gray, the veteran of World War I, warned his audience of the looming storm:

*These are uncertain times. Every hour and every minute is charged with sudden change. Events are happening in every corner of the world that will affect the whole of civilization. Words come daily of war, treachery and human suffering. Now, that all the forces of evil are imposing their will on the forces of good, we are on trial for the faith that is in us. If we are to combat this menace successfully, we must stand together and hold fast all the institutions which we have built up in our saner moments. The GSA is one of these institutions.*

John Gray was walking a bit of a tightrope. As a Canadian, with his country already at war, he was presiding over a largely American association in a country that was trying to stay out of that same war. We know of course where veteran Gray's sentiments were, but he had to keep his personal feelings in the background. As for the Americans, Pearl Harbor was still some time away.

Under the circumstances, Gray came up with solid advice for his greenkeeping constituents:

> Now that the forces of evil are imposing their will on the forces of good, we are all on trial. Now more then ever, we need to respect each other. We need to cooperate and forget envy and suspicion. Pretty (sic) jealousies should promptly be dismissed and a sincere effort made to pull together.

The 1941 GSA Conference was held in Detroit at the Book-Cadillac Hotel February 4–7. The impressive educational program included Horace Purdy who spoke about his troublesome weeds at the Toronto GC and Mr. C.H. Smith, the Green Chairman of the Essex GC. Others included such well known names as Dr. Fred Grau, Dr. Tyson, and Dr. Monteith of the USGA. During the early conferences the educational sessions were always in the afternoon with visits to the exhibits planned for the morning. The concluding banquet with appropriate entertainment was a grand affair, but the evening belonged to John Gray. At one point, John's son Lyle got hold of the microphone on the podium and sang songs to the much bemused audience. Lyle must have been quite a singer because he brought the house down with his rendition of Old Man River. The old man, sitting on his throne with a tear in his eye and his lovely Evelyn at his side, must have been touched. He was 56 years old.

At the annual meeting of GCS, John Gray stood for

reelection but he faced a tough opposition from Harold Stodola, a university-educated superintendent from Minneapolis. Such presidential elections are quite unusual in the annals of the superintendents' movement. In fact, none has happened before or since. It would seem that there may have been some political maneuvering in the ranks of the GSA, but there is no evidence to substantiate that. In addition to the presidential runoff, the nominating committee had also placed the names of six well-known superintendents on the floor of which only three would be elected. Among the six was Eb Steiniger, the superintendent at Pine Valley GC in New Jersey. Steiniger was born and educated in Germany. Steiniger's biography listed his hobby as "Staying single."

Gray, the gruff-looking farmer superintendent, was defeated by handsome Harry Stodola, the new breed of college-educated superintendent. Steiniger was not elected either, possibly because he was of German background at a time when the U.S.A. was about to go to war with that country. Another possibility could be that he flaunted his single lifestyle in the conservative community of his colleagues. As an afternote, Stadola became the only GSA president who served for five years, because there were no conferences or elections during World War II. An interesting thought occurs: if Gray had defeated Stodola, what would the American reaction have been to having a Canadian at the helm for five years?

For John Gray, the summer of 1941 was a return to the reality of greenkeeping from the hoopla of having been president of his professional association. It was not a difficult transition. John Gray loved his work. He worked diligently and planted trees among the fairways, nurtured the saplings, and tended his precious greens to perfection.

Within his community, Gray was considered an expert. He often advised on golf course maintenance, architecture, and construction. He had a good eye for golf courses according to his son Lyle. He could pick out a problem right away. Nick Panasiuk, who operated a golf course near Windsor, knew John Gray well and testified that the old greenkeeper never turned down requests to help.

At Essex, the members were equally proud of their talented greenkeeper and honored him with a special day on May 17, 1952 to celebrate his many contributions to Essex. It was known as "Gray Day." John's longtime friend, Walter Bartlett, who had taken up flying in his later years, landed his small plane on the 11th fairway to call on his old friend. There is no record of the plane leaving marks on the turf, but undoubtedly Gray would have repaired the damage quicker than one could cut a green.

Gray had given unselfishly to Essex GC, often to the detriment of his own health. The heart of this big man, 6' 2" and 250 lbs., finally gave out on Thanksgiving Day, 1958. Born on a farm near Aberdeen, Scotland in 1885, he was 73 years old when he died.

He left behind a wife and two children and a legacy of achievements and improvements to the Essex GC. Some years later, when the American architect Arthur Hills was asked to modernize the golf course, he wisely left the greens alone. According to Hills, "The greens at Essex were the best set of greens ever created by the great Donald Ross." With that statement Hills joined a large number of prominent people who conveniently forgot the hard work, the dedication, and the expertise of possibly Canada's best all-time greenkeeping superintendent, one of the greatest of our unsung heroes.

# *Historical Footnote:*

1940: GSA member Fred Coulson, greenkeeping superintendent at the Roseland GC in Windsor, Ontario, gave up greenkeeping to become an instructor of pilots for the RAF.
Coulson was a pilot in World War I, was shot down, and
turned to greenkeeping as a profession afterward to help build
up his health. Since he was in his country's service, his dues
were automatically suspended in the GSA and the Michigan
& Border Cities Association.

# CHAPTER V

# 1940–1970
# World War II and the
# Early Growth of Golf

"Greenkeeper Bob Anderson is to maintain his membership and remain in good standing while he serves
overseas." So it was moved and carried at a meeting of the
Ontario Greenkeepers Association in 1940. At a later meeting
it was further decided that 300 cigarettes be send to Bob Anderson from his friends.

Only a few of the greenkeepers in Ontario joined the
armed forces overseas; those that did earned the widest respect and retained their memberships in the association. The
war put a damper on golf and greenkeeping, but not to the
same extent as had been the case during World War I. Existing
courses continued to maintain their grounds and no new facilities were developed.

The start of World War II also spelled the end of an era for the Ontario Greenkeepers Association. Sansom had abdicated several years earlier and Hawkins was to give up the reigns in 1941. He was succeeded by John Austin of the Humber Valley GC, who was well prepared since he had acted as secretary for several years and was familiar with the workings of the group. He could still call on either Sansom or Hawkins since both men continued to attend the regular meetings for several years to come.

On occasion Austin would call a meeting at his home in Thistletown to deal with special problems such as the dues of William Kirby, the greenkeeper at Lambton and one of the original members who had been present at the Weston GC in 1924. Bill Kirby had fallen in arrears and did not respond to repeated notices asking him for payment. It was a ticklish situation made more complicated by the fact that Kirby had fallen on hard times at Lambton GC. The club had hired Dick Homewood to replace Kirby. How was the new president to deal with this situation? He resolved the problem neatly by making Kirby an honorary member and admitting Homewood into the fold as an associate member.

Homewood quickly advanced to secretary and then president in 1948, a position he held for two years. It was also during the early 1940s that longtime greenkeeper Bill Pritchard from Thornhill was succeeded by Alex McClumpha. Pritchard left for the Royal Ottawa but not before becoming an honorary member. McClumpha quickly joined the association as a director as did his son Bill. Alex McClumpha married a much younger woman who was the bookkeeper at Thornhill. Margaret McClumpha later served for a while as the secretary for the greenkeepers association. While Alex McClumpha was already in his late 60s, his wife Margaret gave birth and his colleagues teased old Alex about the fact that at the same time as he was receiving the old age pension he was also collecting the baby bonus.

The end of the war marked the end of John Austin's presidency. Dick Homewood succeeded him in 1948. During that time, meetings were often held at the homes of various directors. Just as often, the boys drank a case or more of beer and the minutes record that the beer was paid for "out of funds." Presumably that meant out of the association kitty. Not everyone agreed with this practice! Horace Purdy in particular took exception. Perhaps, for that reason, Purdy refused to pay his dues and on various occasions Purdy was threatened with expulsion for non-payment. He actually lost his membership for a while, but was voted back in in 1946. Also in that year, Keith Nisbet and Art Price joined the group. Both men were to play influential roles in future years. Art Price had bought a 9-hole course in Credit Valley and became not only a member but also a benefactor to the group. He often made his clubhouse and his course available for meetings and functions and lent support by attending meetings and giving advice. At a time when greenkeepers generally were still very much second class citizens in the framework of golf, the support and friendship of Art Price and Keith Nisbet, both owners of golf facilities, were very important.

In 1946, the association was giving thought to organizing a golf tournament for its members. At a meeting in June 1946, the members agreed to award three prizes to greenkeepers three to assistants, and one prize to greenkeepers over 50 years of age. They further decided that the Ontario Greenkeepers Association was to be the governing body of the tournament and that the tournament committee be appointed by the president of the association. Support was sought from within other areas in the provinces. Both Jim Hickman in London and Snider at Westmount were approached. The tournament was to be known as the Alex McClumpha Tournament, open to all greenkeepers and one assistant per club. The first tournament was conducted in 1947 at the Thornhill GC and the association contributed $50 in prize money to help make it a success. The Alex McClumpha Tournament became an annual event after that inaugural meeting and never missed a year in its long history that has extended to contemporary times.

Meanwhile, there seems to have been a falling-out between John Austin and Dick Homewood. Austin wanted to organize an equipment field day at his Humber Valley GC but the directors wanted no part of it. It was suggested instead that equipment could be exhibited during the McClumpha Tournament, which did not satisfy Austin. He resigned in a huff and the association accepted his resignation. Dick Homewood was not very happy about the situation and decided that three years of being president were enough. He was presented with a set of pipes as a token of appreciation for his efforts.

By now, Jack Abbott, had returned from Rosedale to his first course, the course which his family had owned and on which he held a mortgage for a longtime—the Islington GC. Abbott was in charge for four years from 1950–1952. During that time, Horace Purdy became the delegate for the Ontario chapter and carried as many as 15 votes to the annual meeting of the American association. That number was a substantial reduction from before the war when all Ontario Greenkeepers Association members automatically belonged to the national association in America. Apparently the dual membership requirement was abandoned without notice. At the election at the U.S. conference, Abbott was voted in as director of the American body and served for two years, but Abbott confided to this author many years later, that he felt out of place at their meetings and had little in common with his American colleagues.

During this time, regular exchange meetings were conducted with the Western New York State Golf Superintendents Association at which superintendents toured each other's courses and discussed grass and greenkeeping. One year the Buffalo boys would come to Toronto and the next year a return visit would be made by the Canadians to Buffalo. Arthur Stephen, superintendent at the Erie Downs GC in Fort Erie, was instrumental in facilitating these exchanges. These meetings were to continue on an irregular basis into the 1970s, but have since ceased.

During the summer of 1949, a special meeting was called to arrange the third annual McClumpha Tournament. It was decided that the first prize would be $25.00 and a cup. There was to be a special handicap flight for seniors in which first prize was also $25.00. There were further money prizes for coming in second and third. It is worth mentioning that the annual dues at the time were still only $5.00.

That year the November meeting was again held at the home of Jack Abbott and the entire board was re-elected by acclamation. (Of course it would have been difficult to vote against one's host!) At the annual meeting it had become customary to audit the books of the association, usually by two upright and capable members. In 1949 these two members were Keith Nisbet and Art Price. Since there were only a few hundred dollars and often less involved, the task was not a huge assignment and Nisbet and Price found the books to be in good order. It was further decided to return to the Walker House on Front Street for December with the stipulation that no refreshments be served until a vote had been taken. Memories of rowdy meetings at the Royal York Hotel were still fresh in the minds of some. Under the subtle prodding of

Keith Nisbet, booze and drinking became less of an issue at meetings, at least when Keith was around.

In December of 1950, the association made a momentous decision to change its name from Ontario Greenkeepers Association to Ontario Golf Course Superintendents Association. Some suggested that Quebec be included since there was no association of greenkeepers in that province. At a later meeting that spring, Horace Purdy and Dick Homewood moved that the name be changed to Canadian Golf Course Superintendents Association. That motion was carried unanimously. Secretary Bill Forrester from the Weston GC was instructed to act on this motion and in the July minutes of that year, it is reported that the name change had been accepted. But that announcement proved to be premature. The provincial secretary had reservations and the association once more filed its annual returns under its old name.

In the spring, the association had to deal with another difficult problem. Joe Peters and Joe Roberts both of whom claimed to be the greenkeeper at the Oshawa GC, had applied for membership. The bylaws clearly stated that only one greenkeeper per club could be accepted as a member. What to do? After an investigation by George Darou, it was decided to accept Joe Roberts as a new member from Oshawa GC and that Joe Peters would be an unaffiliated member. The latter would later take a position at the Strathroy GC. Joe Roberts at Oshawa became a very supportive member who served on the Board of Directors at various times and hosted many meetings at his club.

As a result of these difficulties Bill McClumpha was asked to overhaul the bylaws of the association, a task for which he was well qualified since he would shortly become the manager at the IBM GC near Unionville.

In 1952, the dues were raised from $5.00 to $10.00.

*Dr. Fred Grau and Tom Unsworth, 1960.*

Total income in 1951 had been only $160 (with 32 members) and expenses had totaled $216. Obviously, the association could not continue to run at a deficit and the dues increase was approved, but it was not enough. A few months later the association levied a special assessment of $5.00 to look after a shortfall. Also for the first time, the association accepted associate members. Their annual fee was also $10.00 but associate members could not vote.

In 1952, Jack Widgett from York Downs and Bill Aimers from Rosedale became new members. Aimers was only the second college-educated superintendent. The first was Horace Purdy at Toronto Golf. Aimers took over from Jack Abbott at Rosedale but lasted only a year. He was an entrepeneur at heart and quickly established himself as a successful businessman in the golf course industry. Widgett's career at York Downs was equally short-lived. Norman McDonald, who stayed at York Downs until the club moved from Downsview to Unionville in 1970, succeeded him.

At the end of this busy year, at a meeting in November, Alex McClumpha was elected unanimously as president and Bill Calhoun from the Pine Point GC was made secretary/ treasurer. Although the Pine Point GC has long since been subdivided, the club house with its distinctive Tudor gables has become a landmark on the north side of the 12-lane 401 Highway north of Toronto.

The new regime of Alex McClumpha moved forward decisively: no more meetings in the Walker House in downtown Toronto. The good old days had come and gone once and for all. Instead, the superintendents opted for the meetings to be held at golf clubs such as the IBM CC where the welcome mat was always laid out. It was also decided that the annual dinners had to be paid for by members individually, instead of out of general funds. The same with drinks. That was the end of free booze.

In 1953, David Moote and Art Dodson became members. Dave Moote had taken over from Bill Aimers at Rosedale and Art Dodson had become the new superintendent at the Summitt GC. The latter course had become vacant when McDonald took over from Jack Widgett at York Downs. Another new face on the Toronto scene was Lloyd Reilly who for many years had looked after the Cutten Club in Guelph, where he had become a disciple of Stanley Thompson. When Thompson designed a new course in Downsview, Reilly became the superintendent.

# The O.A.C. at Guelph

The threat of having Quebec superintendents belonging to the Ontario association must have stirred the boys in La Belle

Province. In the fall of 1953, they organized their own group. And on December 13 of that same year, the secretary of the Ontario Golf Course Superintendents Association was instructed to send a letter to the newly formed Quebec group, wishing them well.

It was not only the Quebec association that was getting its feet off the ground. The OAC was finally getting serious about establishing some turf plots at the college. Both the RCGA and the Ontario Golf Course Superintendents had been prodding the Department of Horticulture and its department head, Dr. Shoemaker, to do some turf research work. Many promises were made but nothing significant really happened until the persistent efforts of Ralph Goodwin-Wilson, a professor in the Horticultural Department, finally yielded results. In retrospect we cannot but wonder what all the fuss was about. The grass plots in question hardly measured a few hundred square feet. They were located to the south of the greenhouses near a pretty lily pond. This author at times studied the different grasses while attending college in Guelph (1954–58). The plots were certainly not impressive and often neglected, but they were a beginning of better things to come. The superintendents learned early that Guelph and the government moved slowly at the best of times and not at all during adverse economic times.

Annual turf conferences at the College had been organized since 1947 and they were held in the middle of March in a large lecture hall in the Horticultural Department. It was here that Ontario superintendents and greenkeepers were for the first time exposed to the likes of Dr. Tyson from MSU, Dr. Musser from Penn State, and Fred Grau and Jim Boyce from the Dominion Experimental Farm in Ottawa. Occasionally superintendents were also asked to speak at these winter conferences. Carl Wagner, the superintendent at Lambton GC,

*1955 Superintendents at Guelph.*

was a frequent speaker. The lecture hall in the Horticultural building had a seating capacity of about 200. At the front of the room was a raised platform, none too stable. Early morning speakers, after a hard night of hospitality at the Royal Hotel in Guelph, often had difficulty finding their balance.

## Annual Dinners

Ever since its inception, the Ontario greenkeepers had organized an annual dinner, a custom that has fallen by the wayside in recent years. The dinner was usually held in a downtown Toronto hotel, often in the afternoon but also in the evening. At first only men participated, but after World War II wives and guests were also invited. Gradually the dinners were moved from the downtown hotels to the country clubs in the suburbs.

With each succeeding year, plans for such dinners became more elaborate. The 1954 version promised to be one of the best. It was to be held at the old St. Andrews GC in Hogs Hollow to the east of Yonge Street in Toronto. For the menu, the superintendents picked a "Turkey Plate," which seemed sensible. Norman McDonald moved, and Art Dodson seconded, that the cost of $2.75 per plate be billed to members present at $3.00, thus taking care of gratuities. Invited guests included Bill Hamilton of the RCGA, Ralph Goodwin-Wilson from the OAC, and all the American speakers, who were in town at the time to participate in the Guelph Conference at the OAC.

Harry Melon, the superintendent at St. Andrews, was authorized to purchase 6 bottles of rum, 12 rye, 6 gin, 3 scotch, 1 bourbon, 4 cases of ale and 2 cases of lager. No doubt the bourbon was for the American visitors; no self-respecting Canadian would drink the stuff. It also appears that Keith Nisbet was losing control (or perhaps he just happened to miss that meeting) and the boys slipped one past him. All that booze was not to be paid for by the association. Members and guests were expected to pay for their own drinks: shots at 50 cents and beer at 25 cents.

## Industrialist E. P. Taylor

A highlight of the summer of 1954 was the decision by the O'Keefe Brewing Company to make a scholarship in golf course maintenance available at the OAC and to seek input from the superintendents. Multimillionaire E. P. Taylor, an ardent golfer, wished to make money available for a deserving student pursuing a career in golf course management. The association wanted to go one step further: it wanted a winter short course for greenkeepers at Guelph and they in turn sought the support of the O'Keefe Brewers.

The short course was a bit premature. It did not happen

until 1972. The scholarship became official but was honored by the brewing company for only a few years. It was a sizeable award—$700, quite a substantial sum in those days. (When the college awarded this author the scholarship in 1958, Mr. Taylor had decided to withdraw the prize.) For a while the wealthy industrialist continued to be a benefactor to the golf course industry, but then his interest shifted to another location. A large portrait-style painting of E. P. Taylor hangs in the men's locker room of the Lyford Cay Club in Nassau, Bahamas. Taylor was the founder of that club and played golf there for the remainder of his life.

## Another Banquet

The 1955 annual banquet promised to be even bigger and better than the 1954 version. Now Harry Melon was authorized to purchase even more booze: 8 bottles of rum, 16 bottles of rye, 8 of gin, 4 scotch, still only 1 bottle of bourbon, and 4 cases of beer—more than three cases of hard liquor and four boxes of beer. This time the executive settled on a chicken dinner for $2.50 which was charged back to the members at $2.75.

For a small association with fewer than 100 members, this seems like an awful lot of liquor, we must remember that guests and wives were also invited. There were no ride programs and the dangers of drinking and driving had not become as big an issue as it has today. The fact remains that in the early days heavy drinking was much more part of everyday life than it is in contemporary days. Although Keith Nisbet was by no means a teetotaler, he did frown on excessive drinking and he encouraged his colleagues to practice moderation. As usual, he was ahead of his time. Few listened. Witness the following drinking song, which the boys could be heard singing after they had tippled a few.

# A TOASTE

Booze, oh booze, you are my guest,
You oft times keep me from my rest
You oft times make me wear old clothes
You always make my friends my foes
But see you are so near my nose
I'll tip you up, and down she goes!

(Contributed by Dudley Smith, Chicago golf superintendent who sang this song with his Canadian colleagues at the time of the 1961 GCSAA Conference at the Royal York Hotel in Toronto.)

Besides organizing banquets and meetings and drinking a lot, the association did many other good things such as sending flowers and fruit baskets to sick members and making contributions to charities. The OGSA regularly contributed to such charities as the Mentally Retarded Children, Muscular Dystrophy, and the Salvation Army.

During the ensuing years, golf course construction accelerated all over Canada and the superintendents association grew likewise. Conferences drew a larger attendance and soon the lecture room in the Horticultural building at Guelph became too small. Several other buildings were tried at the OAC, but the move to a bigger center became inevitable. The RCGA took the conference to the Skyline Hotel in Mississaugua and a timely move it was. More and more out-of-province superintendents attended the Toronto conference, which ultimately lead to the formation of the Canadian Golf Superintendents Association in 1966.

(See addendum: History of the CGSA)

# Golf Course Maintenance
# After the War

The 75th anniversary booklet of the Toronto Ladies GC contains an interesting passage about the problems the course was having with weeds.

> *The weeds on the course were a horrendous problem, made worse by the clay-dominated soil and poor irrigation. Superintendent Blake was not much of an agronomist either. We wanted him to grow turf, but all that Blake grew were weeds, weeds. One of the members got so mad, she really bawled him out, but it really made no difference. Blake was a grim, severe man, not easy to get along with.*

If Joe Blake had only had a supply of 2-4D, the magic weed killer that had been discovered just prior to the war and was gradually becoming available to the golf course industry, it would have solved his problems. Of course it is possible that the Ladies GC, which always had a reputation for extreme frugality, did not wish to spend any money on fancy sprayers and weed killers. Therefore, they were destined to hand weed the fairways and the greens until economic times improved. This they did on many occasions with many of the members participating. Blake survived but became even grouchier with the passing of time.

According to Jim Watson from the Toro Company and several other experts, the invention of 2-4D was by far the most significant development in turf culture during the first half of the twentieth century. Weeds had been a big problem at the Toronto GC and may have led to the premature departure of Superintendent Sansom. Many other courses suffered likewise and weeds may also have contributed to Joe

Blake's stern personality, but eventually the magic chemical saved his neck.

Grubs were another problem that superintendents had to contend with after the war. Several cycles of June bug infestations damaged golf courses. One of the worst was the summer of 1957, which caused much turf damage in southern Ontario. Fortunately Chlordane proved to be an effective pesticide to control the June beetle grubs. Chlordane was also very persistent in the soil and its effect as an insecticide remained for many years after the chemical was taken off the market by the Department of Agriculture in Ottawa.

Brown Patch and Dollar Spot were recurring problems year after year, but the diseases were mostly a problem on greens. Dollar Spot eventually invaded fairway turf and superintendents were forced to spray their fairway. Kromadt and PMAS were the fungicides of choice.

Protecting turf during the winter against snowmold required a heavy dosage of CaloClor or corrosive sublimate. These powdery materials were mixed with dry sand or with Milorganite for ease of application. The mixing operation involved spreading the fungicide in its powdery form atop a pile of the carrier and shoveling it over several times. The resulting clouds of dust were inhaled by the workers without the least bit of worry and, to the best of our knowledge, not a single person died as a result of the exposure.

The most ravishing plant disease was not on turf but on trees. The Dutch Elm Disease wreaked havoc with the American Elms that were one of the major tree species on Ontario golf courses. All kinds of potions were tried to ward off or to control the Elm Bark beetle but none seemed to work, not even the powerful insecticide DDT. For years, the naked skeletons of the dead American Elms dotted the countryside and these gruesome remnants were also a scar on many golf courses. Few survived and their demise led to a tree planting frenzy that lasted for several decades. In many cases, excessive tree planting programs to replace the Elms have had an adverse effect on the playability of some of our fine old courses.

In terms of equipment, the most significant invention of the post war era was the self-propelled aerator, capable of aerating greens in minutes rather than hours. Tom Mascara, the inventive genius from Pennsylvania, had already invented a verticut machine but his aerator was an instant success and he sold thousands of the machines worldwide. This changed the face of golf course maintenance forever, either for good or for bad, depending on whether one was a greenkeeper or a golfer.

# David Moote, a Leader Ahead of His Time

The Ontario Agricultural College had been a source of talent for the agricultural industry in Ontario and beyond. Most of these young men and women found a place in teaching, research, the government, and private enterprise. Occasionally, one of their graduates would show an interest in turf management. Horace Purdy was the first college educated greenkeeper to be followed by Bill Aimers after World War II. When tall and handsome David Moote graduated from Guelph and took a position as superintendent in 1953, everyone knew that things would never be the same. Dave Moote dominated greenkeeping for the next 25 years. At Rosedale, he quickly started to experiment with different grasses in the nursery. He did not keep his findings to himself. He wrote and talked about what he learned at meetings and conferences. When the Dutch Elm Disease became a huge problem on golf courses, David Moote was one of the first to try injections under the bark of the elm trees. He shared his findings with anyone willing to listen. He was one of our best public speakers. At a time when greenkeepers were still very much kept to the barn, David Moote could be seen talking to the members in the clubhouse. He was an intelligent man with an interesting story and the golfers loved to listen.

At Rosedale, he experimented endlessly with new equipment and new methods. It seemed he was always ripping something up or tearing something down, often to the chagrin of the Rosedale golfers, who wanted things as they had always been. But there was Moote, installing new automatic sprinklers when his colleagues were still watering with hoses. Because of his experimenting and his hard work, Rosedale became known as one of the best maintained golf courses in the province. In the process, David Moote established an enviable reputation for himself which helped advance his career.

David Moote became a member of the OGSA in 1953 and quickly was appointed to the Board of Directors as secretary. In 1959 and 1960 he was only the eighth president of the association. Meanwhile Moote had spread his wings and just like Sansom before him, had become active in the Golf Course Superintendents Association of America. As Sansom had done, he brought the Americans back to Toronto at the venerable Royal York Hotel for their annual conference in 1961. Moote became president of the GCSAA in 1964. It was a proud moment for Canadians and for David Moote.

Shortly after the completion of his presidency, Moote took a superintendent's position at the Essex GC in 1969. He advanced to general manager and was largely responsible for the hosting of a very successful Canadian Open in 1976. David left Essex GC to go to Scarborough GC, where he again became superintendent. Later on he continued his career in Florida for a few more years before retiring.

# George Darou,
# Greenkeeper with a Heart

There were other well-known superintendents from 1950 to 1970 but none of the stature of David Moote. They all deserve mentioning because they made valid contributions. One of the most beloved was George Darou who had come from the Hunt Club in London to a new course in Richmond Hill. Darou had worked with Robert Trent Jones and with Robbie Robinson on the new Hunt Club course. It was therefore no accident that when Robbie Robinson needed a superintendent for the new Richmond Hill course, he called on his friend George Darou. George and his wife Peggy moved to a small bungalow on a rise on Bathurst St. overlooking the course.

Darou was a stalky man of medium height who sported a silvery gray brush cut. His approach to greenkeeping was fundamental and hands-on. He relied on his senses as a means to determine the causes of sick grass. Darou would get down on his hands and knees, peer and pick at the grass, take a small clump, and lift it to his nose. He would sniff the odour and after a pensive moment he would remark: "This smells like fish, and if it smells like fish, you've got problems." Darou had a nose for diseases and he could smell Brown Patch days before the turf actually showed the symptoms. His prognosis of any kind of greenkeeping problem was invariably spiced with earthy remarks that made the listener remember both the diagnosis and the cure. For that reason George Darou became well known and he enjoyed the friendship of his colleagues. Occasionally too much friendship led to troubles such as during the Guelph Turf Conferences. While the lectures in Guelph were conducted at the college, the attendees stayed in hotels in the city of Guelph, such as the Royal Hotel on Wyndham Street. Darou and his friends burned the midnight oil, singing and dancing and drinking till all hours. In the process, they caused some damage to the hotel property and the next year their registration was not accepted and they had to find accommodation elsewhere.

At Richmond Hill, Darou worked hard and diligently and quickly brought the new course to its potential. In the process he earned the respect and esteem from the owner, not just because he was a talented greenkeeper, but also because he had a charming personality. These positive attributes stood Darou in good stead when one spring the Ricmond Hill course suffered a calamity. George Darou had mixed a potent concoction the previous fall containing urea fertilizer and Merfusan fungicide. The weather did not cooperate during the winter. Several mild spells released the synergistic and detrimental effects of the mixture with the result that most of the greens at Richmond Hill were stone dead when spring arrived. Many were reseeded and resodded and golf was delayed for weeks, but there was never any doubt about Darou's position at the club. Only someone as charming and humble as George Darou could survive such a mishap without the obvious consequences. Several years later, he suffered a heart attack and died. His colleagues carried him to the grave.

# Carl Wagner,
# The Man who Conquered the Humber

One other person deserves mention in this era. His name is Carl Wagner. He started his career at the Sunningdale GC in London and then moved to Lambton GC in Toronto. Carl arrived just in time to clean up a terrible mess that nature had spread all over his golf course in the Humber River valley. In October of 1954, Hurricane Hazel struck the Toronto area with excessive rain that flooded many of the low-lying areas in and around the city. The storm raged for several days and nights and finally the rivers were not big enough to contain the raging waters. Flat lands near the rivers were flooded and since it happened unexpectedly, the flood caught many people unaware. Their homes were swept away in the raging torrent and over 100 of the inhabitants drowned in the flood.

Of all the golf courses in the Toronto area, worst hit were the low-lying fairways of the Lambton GC. Wagner and his crew of Italian immigrants went to work immediately after the floodwaters had receded. They removed layers of silt several feet thick, and at times made gruesome discoveries under the mud: Bodies of drowned persons were lodged between the trees and the mud. It was a monumental task but Wagner and his crew, helped by some of the Lambton members, managed to get the course cleaned off and there was only a slight delay for the golfers in the following spring.

Wagner remained at Lambton for many more years. Toward the end of his career he had an unfortunate disagreement with a greens chairman and thought it best to leave. His friend Robbie Robinson, the golf course architect, helped him find a job at the Brudenell GC on Prince Edward Island. From there, he retired to Victoria BC.

# Keith Nisbet, Owner/Operator/Superintendent

Pop Nisbet, a florist in the town of Aurora, had become the owner of the Highland GC on the west side of Yonge St. during the war years. Pop had two sons and a daughter. Son Doug took care of the family flower shop, Keith was placed in charge of the golf course, and their sister married a golf pro, Joe Noble from Thornhill CC.

Keith quickly realized that he needed help with the maintenance of the golf course and he joined the Ontario Greenkeepers Association almost immediately. Once his membership was approved, he missed very few meetings. Beginning in 1944 the name of Keith Nisbet pops up again and again in the annals of the greenkeepers association. It is often said about the benefits of belonging that "one only gets as much as one gives" and Keith Nisbet never tired of giving. In the process he raised the maintenance standards at his own course in Aurora. It gained a reputation as a quality layout providing enjoyable golf to the pay-as-you-play clientele. When Pop Nisbet sold the Highlands, he reinvested his profits in new acreage and with the help of Robert and David Moote developed a 27-hole public golf course (Westview Golf) that set high standards for public golf for years to come.

Keith Nisbet became an innovator and was one of the first to install automatic sprinklers on his course. He also tried new equipment, chemicals, and fertilizers. He often traveled with David Moote to the United States and brought back new ideas, which they implemented on their respective golf courses. Some of the superintendents in the Ontario association felt that Keith Nisbet, being an owner, should not be allowed class A membership in the association. It became a point of contention, but those who got to know Keith quickly realized that he was a greenkeeper at heart and a very knowledgeable one at that. Once the boys found what a gem and a great contributor Keith Nisbet really was, the question of his membership classification was never raised again.

This proud greenkeeper did more than just look after his golf course. He took an active interest in his community, served on committees, on its council, and eventually became the mayor of the town of Aurora. He also served as President of what by that time was known as the Ontario Golf Superintendents Association. For a while he was on the board of directors of the GCSAA in America and undoubtedly would have become president of that group, except that Keith ran into some stiff political opposition that he could not surmount. Instead, he became president of the Ontario Golf Association and in that capacity he probably did more than any other person to help raise the professional image of superintendents in our province. His influence in golf continued long after the term of his OGA presidency expired.

In later years, Keith helped found the Ontario Turfgrass Research Foundation and he continued to support turfgrass endeavors wherever needed. Eventually the work on the golf course became too much and his son Colin took over the responsibility. Pop Nisbet had died some years prior, but a yellow ribbon still hangs in the old oak tree on the back nine of the golf course to remember the old man and brother Doug, who was enamoured by that song.

# The OGSA Presidents 1942–1974

*Side-bar listing OGSA presidents 1940–74*

1936–1941 Fred Hawkins
1924–1935 William Sansom
1942–1947 John Austin
1948–1949 Dick Homewood
1950–1952 John Abbott
1953–1956 Alex McClumpha
1953–1956 Alex McClumpha
1957–1958 Lloyd Reilly
1959–1960 David Moote
1961–1962 Bill Bluett

1963 Tom Unsworth
1964 Art Dodson
1965 George Darou
1966 Keith Nisbet
1967 Robert Moote
1968 S. Gourlay
1969 Allan Jones
1970 John Grightmire
1971 John Arends
1972 William Hynds
1973 James Wyllie
1974 Robert T. Heron

During and after the war, presidents of the association often served for more than just one year. The membership was small and there were not many willing to lead and by default the president often served for extended periods. Austin, Homewood, Abbott, and McClumpha all served multiple terms. Reilly, Moote, and Bluett were each president for a two-year period. In the 1960s interest in the association and attendance at meetings continued to grow and presidents at that time served for only one year.

The name change to Ontario Golf Superintendents Association eventually did take effect in the year 1965. An aspiring young lawyer called Alan Eagleson did the legal work.

Meetings were held monthly, usually in the afternoon, and often a speaker was recruited to do a presentation. Not only the winter meetings but also the summer get-togethers featured a speaker. Thus, there was always an educational component in accordance with the purposes of the association—to promote the exchange of information. At times a few of the superintendents played golf after the meeting, but regular golf outings as part of the meetings never really took off.

In the beginning many superintendents and greenkeepers did not play; others used the age-old excuse that they had no time. The best golfers of that era included Jack Harris, Allan Whitey Jones, and Bruce Woolley. Both were single digit handicap players.

# New Equipment

Occasionally someone organized an equipment demonstration at the monthly meetings. Some marvelous new machinery was invented during that time and put to use on golf courses after the war. The most spectacular new mower was undoubtedly the TORO Parkmaster, which came equipped with seven hydraulically operated mowing units, which could be lifted and lowered with the touch of a finger. The Jacobsen company had their own version of a similar mower: the F-10. The new mowers made it possible for superintendents to cut their fairways as separate units.

On the greens, the riding triplex almost completely replaced the walk-behind greens mower. One triplex could cut all 18 greens in just a few hours thus replacing three to four men with walkers. Both the big fairway unit and the riding greens mowers quickly developed undesirable side effects: tracking of the wheels began to show after just a few seasons and even more quickly on smaller greens. The ugly triplex ring on the greens made it necessary for superintendents to take another look and many eventually switched back to kinder and gentler walkers.

In the sand traps, a Georgia superintendent named Stanley Clarke invented a mechanized trap rake. The first trap rake was colored blue and featured an upright design resembling a moonbuggy. The patent on the new machine was quickly bought out by one of the major manufacturers and

*First annual turf managers short course at University of Guelph, 1970.*

within a few years there were several newer and better models on the market. Raking bunkers by hand, which had been a tedious and repetitious chore, became a thing of the past as most golf courses switched to mechanized raking. There was other machinery, such as topdressing applicators, boom sprayers, and motorized golf carts that either became a blessing or curse, depending on one's point of view.

The early greenkeepers and superintendents relied on their feet to get around the golf course. On flat courses some even used bicycles! Others rebuilt tractors or took the doors off old cars, thereby creating speedy vehicles to get around all 18 holes. Pickup trucks became the vehicle of choice for many superintendents both on and off the course. Wherever a superintendents' meeting was organized, large numbers of pickup trucks could be seen in the club's parking lot.

The introduction of the power golf cart for golfers had a beneficial side affect: they quickly became hand-me-downs in the greenkeeping department and provided a means for the superintendent to get around. The Cushman Company saw an opportunity and built a three-wheeled cart with a box on the back, a sort of motorized wheelbarrow. It was an instant winner in the greens maintenance department of many golf clubs.

With all the new equipment, one would have thought that the number of persons working on the greens crew would have been drastically reduced, but that was not the case. At the same time that new machines were introduced to get the work done quicker, golfers wanted more and more in terms of maintenance, conditioning, and manicuring. Greenkeeping became a balancing act between the demands from the golfers and the needs of the grass. Superintendents faced tough decisions then as now and only the best survived.

## Newsletter

In 1966, the OGSA started a newsletter for its members. It grew quickly from just a few pages to an attractive magazine. When the Canadian Superintendents Association got off the ground in 1966, in a magnanimous gesture, the OGSA donated the magazine and its editor to the CGSA to help the newly formed Canadian group. That's how *The Green Master* was born. More than three decades later, the magazine is still going strong under the same name.

## Other Activities

The need for an educational experience organized by superintendents for superintendents had always been a priority of both the greenkeepers and superintendents since the beginning in 1924. The RCGA-sponsored conference at Guelph had somewhat satisfied that need but it was run by the

WORLD WAR II AND THE EARLY GROWTH OF GOLF

RCGA and golf course superintendents were only invited guests. A one-day symposium was launched in 1967 at the Board of Trade. It was very successful and in the following year a similar event was conducted at the Oakdale GC. Eventually these modest starts led to an annual symposium, first at the University of Guelph and later in Toronto at the Constellation Hotel. But once again, the superintendents had lost control and let a valuable educational medium slip out of their hands.

## The Golden Anniversary 1974

During the summer of 1974, the OGSA proudly celebrated its golden anniversary. Compared to the early days when there were just a few dozen members, the association had become firmly established. There was a healthy bank account and there was no need to go begging to have a party. It was done in style at one of the oldest golf clubs in the city of Toronto— Lambton Golf Club on the banks of the Humber. Host superintendent was Jim Wyllie, who also happened to be president of the Canadian Golf Superintendents Association. Wyllie's former assistant Robert T. Heron was president of the Ontario group. Together these two men organized a fine golf tournament and dinner to which not only superintendents were invited, but also green chairmen and the presidents of various golf clubs. It was a smashing success! In fact the event was such a hit with the OGSA members that it has been repeated annually in one form or another and always draws large crowds.

The guest of honour was the oldest living member of the OGSA, Dick Homewood, who was a charter member and the association's fourth president. Homewood spent his retirement years as a gardener at the Lambton GC.

*A distinguished group of visitors graced the head table at the golden anniversary of the Ontario Golf Course Superintendents Association at Weston. L to R are Golf Course Superintendents of America President Charles Baskin of Waterbury, Conn., Ontario President Bob Heron of Markland Wood, GCSAA Vice–President Palmer Maples Jr. of Atlanta's Standard Golf Club, and Dr. Clay Switzer, Dean of the Agronomy Department at the University of Guelph. Printed from* Teeoff *Dec. 13, 1974.*

Guest speaker after the dinner was Dr. Clayton Switzer, Dean of Agriculture at the University of Guelph. Switzer was later to become Deputy Minister of Agriculture. As a teacher at Guelph in Botany and Weeds, Clay Switzer became a friend of all superintendents. Not only did he teach us in a unique and understanding way, he also played golf with the superintendents and he influenced the powers at Queens Park to treat our industry benignly. The OGSA eventually rewarded Dr. Switzer with an honorary membership and a set of quality golf clubs.

# Influential Threesome

A report on the festivities at Lambton was written up in the September 1974 issue of *The Green Master* by David Gourlay who had taken over as editor of the magazine in 1973. Gourlay, who had served as president of both the OGSA and the CGSA, was part of the powerful triumvirate that included Bob Heron and Jim Wyllie. These three men dominated the direction that greenkeeping had taken not only in Ontario but also to some degree in Canada. In fact, Wyllie's powers extended beyond the borders of Canada. He became the president of the American association as well. Individually, all three served as president of the OGSA and as president of the CGSA. They were active in *The Green Master* magazine and they also managed with the help of Sid Puddicombe from Alberta to take a very successful annual conference awayfrom the RCGA and make it the property of the superintendents in Canada, a move that put the CGSA on sound financial footing.

*Lambton Superintendent Jim Wyllie (right) congratulates 85-year-old Veteran Dick Homewood.*

The influence of these three men was far-reaching and their hard work and dedication were largely responsible for both the

OGSA's and the CGSA's success from 1970 to 1980. David Gourlay was recognized by the GCSAA with its Distinguished Service Award and by the CGSA with the John B. Steel Award. Heron received the Score Award in recognition for his achievements. Wyllie gained fame and fortune as an entrepreneur and a consultant. His major contribution to the Bayview GC was the fairway conversion from Poa annua to bentgrass. Wyllie used the scorched earth technique, which involved spraying all the fairways with glyphosate or Round-up and slit seeding with bentgrass. This method was copied under Jim Wyllie's direction at several other courses, including St. Georges, Burlington, and Look-out Pointe GC. All three of their sons have gone on to be successful superintendents.

# CHAPTER VI

# Boom Times
# 1975–2000

In the mid-1960s three new courses were built in the greater Metropolitan Toronto area which would have a major impact on the golfing scene in the province for years to come. Quebec architect Howard Watson designed all three. The first one was the spectacular 36-hole Board of Trade Country Club. Constructed in the Humber Valley near Woodbridge, it quickly gained acclaim and was the site of the 1967 Carling World Championship, a Canadian centennial tournament. At the same time Watson was building the Board of Trade, he was busy at the nearby Pine Valley GC. When he completed both courses, he was called upon to lay out yet another 18-hole course near the Sixteen Mile Creek in Oakville, which became known as the Upper Canada Country Club.

All three courses Watson designed had one thing in common: severely sloping greens, a Howard Watson trademark. The greens often surface-drained in three different directions and it was not uncommon for elevation differences to exceed five, six, seven, and even more feet. The severity of the greens created a love-hate reaction among the golfers who chose to play on these courses. At the Board of Trade many of the greens were reshaped with the passing of time. At the Pine Valley Course there was a change of ownership and the new owner, Gill Blechman, influenced by what he had seen at the Butler National in Chicago, hired Tom Fazio to completely rebuild the course. The result was the magnificent National Golf Club, which has been the top-ranked course in Canada since *Score Magazine* instituted national rankings.

In Oakville, golf promoter/entrepreneur, Reg Acomb, struggled with the Upper Canada CC for several years and then, through luck or circumstance, managed to promote a relationship with the RCGA. The golf association in turn hired Jack Nicklaus to build a championship course for the Canadian Open named Glen Abbey GC. Acomb stayed on as project manager with Dennis Pellrene as the overseeing superintendent. When the project was completed, Dennis remained superintendent as did his assistant Sid Witteveen.

Pellrene had started his career on the sand greens of Alberta, moved to the St. Catharines GC as assistant to John Piccolo, and received a major break when Acomb chose him to help build Glen Abbey. The construction and maintenance of the Abbey was state-of-the-art and drew the attention of everyone in the industry. Although Penncross Bentgrass was the predominant grass used for greens at the time, under the influence of Nicklaus it was decided to use C-15 stolonized bent on the greens. It was probably the last time that this method of green establishment was to be used in the province or perhaps, in the country. The stolons were obtained from Warren Turf Nurseries near Chicago. The same nursery also supplied the C-15 turf to several new golf courses in the U.S.A. including the Fazio-designed Butler National and the Muirfield course in Ohio. Ironically, C-15 originated in Toronto and was variously known as Scarborough or Toronto Bent. It may have been an offshoot of the Washington Bentgrass first introduced by Dr. Piper in 1922 to Toronto GC or it may have been propagated from a naturally occurring Bentgrass on the Scarborough GC near the Highland Creek.

The new greens at Glen Abbey established quickly. For the first few years, both the greens and the golf course were praised by the players, but all was not well. Gradually the turf developed stress symptoms of thinning out for no reason. Conventional fungicides did not help. Michigan State University was asked to look into the matter and research the mysterious disease. Dr. Joe Vargas did eventually find a cure for what became known as "C-15 Decline," but it was not in time for the Canadian Open in the summer of 1981.

The golf course in Oakville was in less than perfect condition when Jack Nicklaus came to inspect his masterpiece. The greens particularly were suffering and Nicklaus was not pleased. Nor did Nicklaus hide his displeasure. "The greens and the fairways? They both stink," said Nicklaus in the *Toronto Star* at the time. He was no more complimentary in the *Globe and Mail*. It was intimated and indeed suggested widely that "the greenkeeper should be fired." Such undue criticism did not inspire the hard-working greens staff at Glen Abbey. According to Pellrene, the workers were really upset and "ready to walk." That would have been disastrous and detrimental to the conclusion of the tournament.

Nicklaus got wind of the rumblings and became concerned that he had perhaps gone too far with his criticism. He decided to make amends and paid a visit to the old white barn at Glen Abbey near the 17th green to address the greens crew.

Nicklaus spoke softly, according to Mike Van Beek who was in attendance, and he alleged that he had been misquoted and that he really appreciated the hard work of the greens workers. That pacified the situation somewhat, but the damage had been done. Pellrene worked hard to restore the greens by overseeding continuously with Penncross. The course was never closed during the overseeding process but all the hard work was not enough to save Pellrene's neck. The Nicklaus group maintained that, "their C-15 at Muirfield showed no signs of stress," implying that not the grass, but the management at Glen Abbey was at fault.

The RCGA needed a scapegoat and in the fall, 1981, Jordie Hilton, the RCGA Executive Director, fired Pellrene. Within two years, the turf at Muirfield also gave up the ghost to the bacterial wilt. That course was closed for an entire season and the greens gassed and replanted with a new grass.

Pellrene fared much better than his grass. He was quickly snapped up by the Scarborough GC, a course that badly needed his talents. The members at Scarborough appreciated his efforts and were sorry to see him leave ten years later for the Capilano GC in Vancouver. From the depths of despair, after having been fired from Canada's best-known golf course, Pellrene's star rose to greater heights than he had ever dreamed of. In the spring of 2000, he received the Score Award, as Canada's Superintendent of the Year—this very same golf course superintendent who had once been thought inadequate for Canada's prime course, the Glen Abbey in Oakville.

At Glen Abbey, Pellrene was succeeded in quick succession by Don McFaul and Paul White, both of whom stayed for only a few years. Dean Baker has been in charge for the past decade. The golf course meanwhile recovered from the C-15 blight and has been in remarkable condition ever since Pellrene's problems in 1981.

The only exception is the 11th green, located in the valley across Sixteen Mile Creek. The infamous 11th is in a difficult location with shade in the morning and hot sunshine in the afternoon and very little air movement for the rest of the day. The green has been rebuilt several times and although it looks spectacular every spring, by tournament time the grass is usually sparse. In the spring of 2000, Dean Baker rebuilt the green for the fifth time, using a completely new mix and a new grass cultivar called L-93.

## Superintendents at Glen Abbey

| | |
|---|---|
| Dennis Pellrene | 1977–1981 |
| Don McFaul | 1982–1987 |
| Paul White | 1988–1989 |
| Dean Baker | 1989–current |

## Others Follow Suit

Because of the success experienced by the pace-setting National, the Board of Trade and Glen Abbey Golf Courses, developers all over our province got bitten by the golf bug. New courses sprang up from Windsor to the Quebec border and from Niagara to Thunder Bay. New golf courses designed by both American and Canadian architects dotted the landscape in ever increasing numbers. Everyone wanted part of the action and while most new golf courses did well, there were a few that floundered. Invariably, these very same golf courses that did not make it the first time were picked up by new investors and, under new ownership, they prospered.

At the same time, OGSA membership grew by leaps and bounds and the regional associations also increased their numbers.

In August of 1984, the OGSA celebrated its 60th anniversary. Once more it was time for a party, but a party with an interesting twist. A threesome of OGSA past presidents, Bob Moote (1976), John Arends (1971), and Allan Jones (1969), came dressed in golf attire from 1924. The threesome wore knickers and were equipped with hickory shafted clubs. They led off the tournament of Green Chairman, Club President, and Superintendent at the Sunningdale GC near London. It was a spectacular sight and the sounds of pipes and drums leading the three golfers to the tee added a dramatic dimension. The pomp and circumstance mesmerized everyone. Amazingly, none of the golfers succumbed to first tee jitters. All drove it straight down the middle. Another milestone conquered, another achievement in the annals of the OGSA.

The following year, the Superintendent/Green Chairman Tournament was at the Board of Trade in Woodbridge. Walter Woods, Links Supervisor from St. Andrews, Scotland, attended the event and was the guest of honour and the after dinner speaker.

# The Ontario Turfgrass Research Foundation

The OTRF was created by Paul Dermott, who, with great assistance from Keith Nisbet, Alan Beeney and others, organized fundraisers. With money in hand, Paul Dermott, Keith Nesbit, and Des Rice, President of the Weedman, met with officials from the Ontario Department of Agricultural and pushed the college in Guelph to take action. Land was made available in Guelph near the university, a building was erected, and grass plots established—the Guelph Turfgrass Institute was born. The superintendents received support from the sod growers,

*OGSA Field Day, 1990.*

*Guelph Turfgrass Institute, June 12, 2000. Home of the OGSA.*

landscapers and lawn sprayers headed by the aggressive Des Rice. The cooperation of this dynamic group, manifested at the University of Guelph, led to a higher profile for the turf-grass industry as a whole, and especially the status of the su-perintendents' profession.

The first fundraising efforts originated at a golf tourna-ment at the National Golf Club. Superintendent Ken Wright influenced owner Gill Blechman to donate the golf course for a day. The tournament was followed by a picnic at the Board of Trade Turf Care Center. This select combination at-tracted more than 100 avid golfers, keen to play the Na-tional. At the social picnic after the tournament, nearly double that number attended the festivities. Special guests from the United States attended, thus making the tourna-ment and the picnic the premier event of the season, some-thing not to be missed! The food, the beer and wine, the salad, the veggies and even the prizes, were all donated. This highly successful event raised more than $10,000 annually and continued for nine years without interruption and with-out ever being rained on. This initial influx of seed money was all that was needed to get the OTRF off the ground. Soon money from many other sources flowed into the treas-ury. It was not uncommon for clubs to donate a dollar per year per member to the OTRF in support of turfgrass re-search. The Board of Trade has donated more than $1500 annually since the program began. Weston GC, Bayview GC, and several others did the same.

The single largest donation came from longtime CGSA member Mac Frost and his wife Elizabeth, who made avail-able more than a half-million dollars, enough to erect a spa-cious research and teaching center near the university. The Frosts operated a multiple course operation near Stouffville,

Ontario and have been longtime supporters of turfgrass research at the University of Guelph.

# OGSA Presidents

*Side Bar of OGSA Presidents:*

1975 Paul Dermott
1976 Paul Dermott
1977 Allan Beeney
1978 Pelino Scenna
1979 Stuart Mills
1980 Paul White
1981 Ken Nelson
1982 Bob Brewster
1983 Rusty Workman
1984 Al Draper
1985 Hugh Kirkpatrick
1986 Barry Endicott
1987 Robert Kennedy
1988 Thom Charters
1989 Neil Acton
1990 Gordon Nimmo
1991 Mark Hagen
1992 Rhod Trainor
1993 David W. Gourlay
1994 Bruce Burger
1995 John Taylor
1996 Alex Labelle
1997 Simon George
1998 Ian Bowen
1999 Ian Bowen
2000 Keith Bartlett

# Regionalization

In 1980, the OGSA directors felt that the make-up of the board should reflect the geography of the province and so the four regions were created, each with two directors. Attendance at meetings had been dwindling and it was thought that regionalization would revitalize the association. It was a dream that did not come true. Attendance continued to decrease but surprisingly a number of regional associations sprang up. The Georgian Bay group, Ottawa Valley Turfgrass Association, the eastern Ontario group, and the southwest organization, had their start during this period from 1980 onward. The western group continued on its merry way with popular and well attended meetings.

The OGSA reduced the number of its meetings as fewer and fewer people showed up. It seemed that many superintendents wanted to join the OGSA and feel part of this dynamic group, but few were willing to give time to the association and attend the meetings. The regionalization of the OGSA was given up at the annual meeting in the year 1997 under the presidency of Ian Bowen.

The one meeting that never lacked for interest and attendance was the April meeting in Windsor, often in conjunction with the Michigan Border Cities group. This was the old

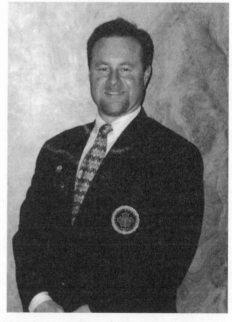

*Ian Bowen, President 1998–1999.*

John Gray group of the 1940s, which had been rejuvenated by Danny Uzelac, owner/operator of the Dominion GC. Danny and his wife Dorothy hosted the April meeting for a number of years very successfully. It attracted large numbers of both American and Canadian superintendents. The habit of trekking to Windsor in April became so entrenched, that when the Uzelacs sold their golf course, the boys just kept on going from force of habit.

A yearly meeting in June at the Galt CC, hosted by popular superintendent Pelino Scenna and in conjunction with a visit to the turf plots at Guelph, was successful as long as Dr. Clay Switzer and Pelino cooperated. When Switzer retired and Scenna moved to Burlington, the June meeting quickly lost its appeal. That was not the case with the ever-popular Green Chairman/Superintendent Day. There has always been a waiting list for that event.

For many years the OGSA sponsored an annual curling meeting, usually in February or March, but it too suffered from lack of attendance. Annual visits to the University of Guelph turf plots equally have lost some of their former appeal. Perhaps not enough new research is being generated at this experimental site to draw attention. Many feel it is repetitious and not of the same caliber found at Michigan State and Penn State Universities.

The same cannot be said for the ever-popular Turf Managers Short Course, which attracts a full house every year since its inception in 1973. In some years the university sponsored two courses to meet the demand. Since the beginning the short course has graduated more than 2000 students and certainly has had a profound impact on the conditioning of Ontario golf courses. Students from other parts of Canada and even from other countries have also attended. The excellent teaching skills of Dr. Jack Eggens have contributed much to the appeal of the short course as well as having the contributions of his teaching assistant, Norman McCallum.

The Ontario Turfgrass Symposium, started by superintendents in 1967 at the Board of Trade and the Oakdale GC, was organized annually by the OGSA, but eventually taken over by the University of Guelph. It has been an unqualified success and a money winner for both the university and the sponsoring organizations. The sod growers, the landscapers, and the superintendents all learn and their associations share in the proceeds. Just the same, the superintendents lost some of their independence when they affiliated with the university and with the allied associations.

A Christmas party with much dancing and frivolity replaced the annual banquet that had been a highlight during the early years. For a while it was a success but the scare of being caught driving under the influence of liquor kept large numbers away. In recent years there no longer has been a get-together to mark the end of the golfing season. Suitable replacements for the annual banquet and the Christmas party have yet to be discovered.

On their own a small group of superintendents started to play hockey together regularly during the winter months. Participation grew rapidly and resulted in an annual tournament that has attracted as many as ten teams from both the United States and Canada. Recently, Scott Dodson (Park CC, Buffalo) and John Taylor (Twenty Valley GC) have been the driving forces behind this tournament format, which attracted hockey legend Eddy Shack as the guest speaker at the millenium event in Fort Erie, Ont.

For only two successive years, the superintendents on their own organized a William Sansom Memorial Day at the Lions Den in the Village of Woodbridge. It was a social get-together with card playing and some drinks, as in the old days. There were even some toasts to our forefathers. At the last meeting, Kimmo Salonen, superintendent at York Downs, passed around the hat and collected $150 for Ethiopian famine relief. The need to donate to charities has always been characteristic of the superintendents' movement.

The association's newsletter *Green is Beautiful* has reported regularly on the changing scene. Barry Endicott, Superintendent at Nobleton Lakes GC, was one of the early and most creative editors who reported interesting tales in the booklet. Endicott continues to reflect on the past with regular reviews of days gone by. *Green is Beautiful* has won awards and has become a very positive driving force in the association.

# Greenkeeping in Contemporary Times

During the last two decades of this century, two factors affected greenkeeping profoundly: the stimpmeter and the computer. The stimpmeter was introduced by the USGA Green Section and was first demonstrated at the Board of Trade by GCSAA president Mel Lucas during an OTRF function in 1978. Within a few years, many superintendents were comparing green speeds and some even posted the speed of their greens on bulletin boards and in newsletters. The quest for speed became an obsession that eventually affected almost every golf course. Superintendents began to cut their greens even shorter. What had once been a tight quarter became a loose three-sixteenths inch and then the pressure mounted to cut greens at one-eighth of an inch. As if that was not enough, plant breeders developed cultivars that could be cut at less than one-eighth inch. Some superintendents went one step further by double and triple cutting greens. Next, rollers made

*60ᵗʰ anniversary at Sunningdale Golf Club. Alan Jones, Piper, John Arends, and Bob Moote.*

their appearance on putting greens, not heavy wooden or steel drum rollers as in the old days, but light-weight rollers that could literally iron the greens smooth.

Although superintendents often publicly decry the quest for speed, many privately succumb to the pressures of low handicap golfers to provide putting greens at tournament speeds on a daily basis. It was predicted that the stimpmeter would be a passing fad, but that has not been the case. The grooved steel bar seems like a powerful scepter being waved by the god of greenkeeping, urging the practitioners of the age-old profession to provide ever smoother and faster greens. There is also a trend to convert greens to dwarf bentgrass cultivars such as the A and G varieties. Another grass named L-93 is also being used on new greens. For the longest time, Penncross was the premium turf for greens, but its days seem numbered as more superintendents switch to grasses that can be cut shorter and will provide greater speed.

The effect of the computer on greenkeeping was much more gradual at first but in the end it became just as pervasive. The first computers in the turfgrass maintenance facilities were often hand-me-downs from the clubhouse. Superintendents learned to type on computers and to prepare reports for their green committees. They also used computers to keep track of their daily maintenance operations. Preparing and maintaining a budget was an ideal chore with the versatile computer. With the installation of modern irrigation systems came newer and more versatile computers that programmed the sprinklers and the pumphouse. The popularization of the Internet opened up a whole new world in golf course management. Superintendents and assistants and even mechanics had opportunities to exchange information directly and instantly with colleagues at other golf courses beyond our borders.

Our founders, who organized to promote the exchange of information, could not have dreamed what a reality that concept had become. Computers were by no means limited to irrigation systems and the office of the superintendent. Modern sprayers are computer-programmed, making it possible to apply smaller amounts of chemicals more accurately. There is barely a machine in the maintenance arsenal that does not have a computer component of some sort.

At first, it was thought that the future belonged to the young, aggressive superintendents, who were already trained on computers at their schools and colleges. Mature, older superintendents were supposed to fall by the wayside and make room for the new generation. Amazingly, that is not exactly how it happened. Many of the older elite have adapted to the modern age and become computer literate. They handle keyboards with dexterity and interact with one another via the Internet as well as they once did on the telephone. Many of the young lions are waiting patiently on the sidelines for the older supers to retire, just as it has always been.

# New Machinery

Certainly the introduction of many new machines has made life easier for the men and women who now manage our golf courses. From just 50 years ago, when all we had was a fork to punch holes in our turf, there now is a vast array of equipment that will aerate all our turf areas in many different ways, quickly and often almost painlessly, for the golfers. Our sprayers and mowers are much improved. We can do things faster, and more efficiently. But surprisingly, many of today's superintendents are switching back to doing things the old way. Tees and greens are once again cut with walk-behind mowers. Sand bunkers are now often hand raked. It seems that what goes around, comes around. For a while it seemed as if the triplex greensmower would replace the walk-behind model. Superintendents soon discovered that many of the new machines had their shortcomings and many have switched back to cutting greens the old-fashioned way.

The demise of once familiar chemicals (such as the hydrochlorinated carbons in insecticides and the heavy metals in fungicides), have made it very challenging for superintendents to control diseases. We envy our American colleagues who have so many more products with which to manage their grass. Perhaps we should look to Europe and take note of their stringent regulations on the use of pesticides on golf courses. It seems more likely that in years to come the pendulum will swing toward the European way rather than the American method of disease control. Since the beginning of the Greenkeepers Association in 1924, astute practitioners of the art of growing grass for golf courses have always been

1989 OGSA Board of Directors. Back left to right, Dave Gourlay, Ed Farnsworth, Mark Hagen, Bruce Burger, Mark Schneider, Ted Ellis. Front row left to right John Taylor, Thom Charters, Neil Acton, Gord Nimmo, Rod Trainor.

prepared for change and we have no doubt that the future generation will be just as adaptable as Sansom and Hawkins were in their heydays.

# 75th Anniversary Celebration

In January, 1999, the OGSA began its yearlong 75th anniversary celebration with a cocktail party at the Constellation Hotel in Toronto, just a few miles away from where the association was born in 1924. All past presidents were invited and many attended.

The celebration continued in June with a golf tournament at the Twenty Valley GC with congenial past-president John Taylor as the host. Many other past presidents also participated. The festivities culminated with yet another cocktail party during the Turfgrass Symposium in January, again at the Constellation Hotel. The association had reason to be proud and to celebrate. From its unauspicious beginning in 1924 with just 11 greenkeeping members, it had grown to more than 400 members. The association has become financially sound with a healthy balance sheet. A youthful Keith Bartlet was chosen as president at the annual meeting to ring in the remaining 25 years of the OGSA centenary in 2024. What the future holds, nobody knows, but with so many talented young superintendents now at the helm at numerous courses, there is little doubt that the movement is both upward and forward as it has always been.

# CHAPTER VII

# Our Children and
# Our Friends

For the longest time the greenkeeper's cottage was an idyllic landmark on many a golf course. Some will remember the picturesque small home perched precariously near the 13th tee on St. Georges GC. Herein lived generations of greenkeepers and their families. Jack and Hazel Harris, the Woolleys, and the Hynds all made this small house their home. Summit GC also had a residence available for its greenkeeper near the back of the golf course. At Thornhill the current superintendent's residence served both as the clubhouse and a place to stay for overnight guests. Bill Pritchard and Alex McClumpha, both former greenkeepers at Thornhill, lived in a small two-story building near the 18th tee, which is now used as the superintendent's office. At the old York Downs GC off Bathurst St. in Downsview, Norman MacDonald and his predecessors lived in harmony in a framed cottage near the clubhouse.

The greenkeeper's cottage often came with the property when a farm was converted to a golf course. It had a rustic quality because it had often been an old farmhouse. At times it was built and added onto from leftover materials found near the maintenance shed or the clubhouse. In the beginning green committees thought it would be a good idea for the person who looked after the golf course also to live on the golf course (sort of like the farmer and his cows). The tradition has persisted and to this day many golf courses provide living quarters for their superintendent or their greens staff on the course. For superintendents, living on the course at low rent or no rent has been a way to save some money. But some missed out on the real estate boom when they failed to buy their own home and build up their equity. Most will agree that being on call 24 hours every day, seven days a week can be a bit much. Not having to fight traffic after work does have its advantages and the many children who have grown up on golf courses invariably speak fondly of the experience.

## *Our Children*

In the old days, the greenkeepers cottage had a romantic connotation, but only in the minds of the golfers that passed by. For the people that lived there, it was often another matter.

Cramped quarters and isolation, especially during the winter months, had its drawbacks. David Gourlay, Jr. spent his childhood on the Summit GC. He remembers the long walks from the family home along the 14th hole to Yonge St. so he and sisters could catch a school bus. "It must have been more than a mile," recalls David. Occasionally the children got lucky and caught a welcome ride on their father's pickup truck or one of the greens staff would pick them up. He also remembers golf balls in his bedroom, the result of errant shots by wild golfers. Dave Jr. fondly spoke of playing with the Dodson boys whose father Art was superintendent at nearby Maple Downs GC. When David Gourlay, Sr. moved to Thornhill, and again lived on the golf course property, the walk to school was shortened considerably. Their home was located just west of Yonge St. in the village of Thornhill where it still stands today. David also remembers going out on the course in the evening to check on the sprinklers. The golf environment had a lasting influence on young Gourlay, who pursued a career in golf course management and is now superintendent at a course in Kansas.

Invariably, superintendents who loved their work inspired their children to follow in their footsteps. William Sansom had a son who worked in the pro-shop at Toronto GC. When Sansom laid out a course near Lake Erie, he managed to get his son hired as the professional. Bill Chinery's boys competed in the caddy tournament at York Downs. They won and were on their way to becoming successful professionals in later life. John Gray, in spite of his Scottish ancestry, was a terrible golfer. But he fathered a son who competed against Nick Weslock, twice played in the Canadian Open, and won the mid-amateur championship in California. Few children brought up on or near the golf course have reached such illustrious heights. Most just developed a love for the game and the golf course, and that remained an important part of their lives.

Lorraine Sanderson, *nee* Findlay, also recalls going out with her father Morley, at the Maple City GC in Chatham at night and hearing the click-click of the sprinklers. Lorraine said, "That sound and the stars so clear will stay with me forever. I think the grass gets in your blood." It must have, because Lorraine married one of her father's greens staff and still loves playing golf and being on the course.

Until recently, few women have entered our industry. Unlike Lorraine Sanderson, maybe their fathers never took their daughters out onto the golf course after work. Probably the brightest star who has earned her spurs in the golf course maintenance industry is Nancy Pierce, a graduate from Guelph. After a brief assistantship at the Toronto GC under Bob Brewster, Nancy departed to the Atlantic Provinces as a superintendent. At Links of Crowbush Cove on Prince Edward Island, she demonstrated her abilities and she became a role model for a smattering of young women who are now making their presence felt all across Canada. No book on greenkeeping in the twentieth century would be complete without the mention of the talented Nancy Pierce.

Paul Dermott brought up his family in a home located near the clubhouse on the Chinguacousy GC. The children played with members' kids near the pool and quickly acquired the rich kids' habit of signing for their lunch at the club's snack bar. Dermott put a stop to that just as quickly. Son Vince became a successful superintendent in his own right at the Scenic Woods GC near Hamilton.

John Grightmire, the son of a greenkeeper, lived near the course in Dundas Valley. He learned to play golf from his father and for many years father and son were golfing companions. Years later, John and his wife Laura lived on the golf course at Rosedale and brought up a family of their own. It was a happy period, John recalls, contrasting sharply with the time when I spoke to him about these matters. He was nursing his wife, who was dying of Alzheimer's disease.

Jack Harris, a bear of a man and a gruff one at that, was a longtime greenkeeper and superintendent at some of the best courses in the province. He achieved the dream of every superintendent: he bought a farm and built his very own golf course! His son Jim, who was trained to become a minister, took it over and today runs the successful 27-hole Knollwood operation.

Nick Panasiuk and his wife Victoria built the 18-hole Hydeaway GC near Windsor with their sweat and tears and raised a family in the process. Among their children was one of the most promising juniors in the history of Canadian golf. Under Nick's tutelage this young man won many tournaments both in Canada and abroad. His name was Bob Panasik, who changed his name ever so slightly for whatever reason.

In 1997 Bob Heron organized a golf tournament for father and son superintendents at the Bonaire GC near Coldwater. Beside Bob Heron and his son Scott, almost 20 pairings participated. The father with the most superintendent sons is, of course, Arthur Dodson, who at one time had all three of his offspring in superintendent positions. The tournament was won by Ted and David Decorso from the Victoria Park GC near Guelph, Ont.

The list goes on, but not all stories are joyous with happy endings. Witness the following: Joe Roberts was for many years the greenkeeper at the Oshawa GC. His father had been pro/greenkeeper before him and when the senior retired, Joe was given the choice of becoming either the pro or the greenkeeper. He chose the latter, but when Hal Butler subsequently was appointed professional, Joe never spoke to the new golf pro for all of 40 years. Joe was a miserable, ill-tempered man who threatened to quit every year when he did not get his way. A succession of club officials were all scared to death that Joe would indeed quit. Finally, after many years, a determined green chairman took Joe up on his threat and Joe quit the next day, never to return to the Oshawa GC grounds. He worked for 20 more years at the nearby Winchester GC, where according to fellow workers, Joe's disposition did not improve and he continued to be ornery. Meanwhile, Joe's wife passed away. A few years later in the spring of 1999, Joe Roberts also passed away, but misery followed him beyond the grave. Joe Roberts left an estate in excess of 3 million dollars and willed all of it to charity. He disinherited his only surviving daughter and his grandchildren.

Old-time greenkeepers in their days were exposed to hazardous materials much more so than their contemporary counterparts. Mixing corrosive sublimate, a mercury compound, resulted in clouds of dust that were easily inhaled into the lungs. The dust of DDT was another favorite to which old timers were exposed. Medical researchers have suggested that toxic substances and heavy metals collected into the fatty tissues of the human body can lead to excessive crankiness in later life. In our profession, there are many living examples that give credence to that theory. Old Joe Roberts, God bless his soul, was living proof of that theory.

# Our Friends in the Golf Course Industry

When the greenkeepers first became organized, the group made no room for commercial members. Salesmen and distributors were not allowed to attend meetings. Only in the 1930s were commercial people invited to attend special events. Eventually they were accepted as members, primarily because the association needed their money.

One of the first genuine friends of the association was Blondie Wilson, a sales representative for Webb Seed, a company that not only supplied seed and fertilizer but was also the Toro distributor in the province at the time. Blondie Wilson was knowledgeable about his machinery. He was also a self-taught agronomist, who helped the greenkeepers with their problems. In addition, Blondie was a golfing member at the Mississaugua GC where he got to know Art Dodson, who was an assistant greenkeeper to Bill Bluett. Blondie Wilson helped Art get his first job as superintendent at the Summit GC. Blondie Wilson helped many other greenkeepers not just with sharing agronomic knowledge but also with their professional aspirations. His agronomic knowledge may have been the result of his close relationship with O. J. Noer, the chief agronomist for the Milwaukee Sewerage Commission, the company that produced Milorganite. In the same year that the Ontario Greenkeepers Association was born in Weston, Ontario Milorganite was born in Milwaukee, Wisconsin. O. J. Noer promoted the famous fertilizer for the next 25 years and he did it so effectively that to this day Milorganite remains the product of choice for many superintendents. O. J. Noer visited golf courses all summer long from coast to coast in both Canada and the United States. In the process, he educated the greenkeepers and helped them become superintendents. He spoke intelligently to club officials and in many cases helped the superintendents save their jobs. Nor was he afraid to admonish the greenkeepers if he felt they were at fault. During the winter months, O. J. Noer would hit the conference trail. He rarely missed the Guelph show and his listeners were spellbound by what he had to say.

Other men in that era were Fred Grau and Bert Musser. Fred Grau was one of the first USGA agronomists and Bert Musser was the leading authority at Penn State University. In 1947, Bert Musser wrote a practical and authoritative book on golf course maintenance that remained the bible of the industry for the next 25 years. Both men spoke eloquently at conferences and meetings and were genuine friends of the superintendent. Autographed copies of Bert Musser's books have become expensive collector's items.

Taylor Barnes was the premier salesman for the Spramotor Company in London, the Jacobsen distributor for the province. Barnes drove a black Jaguar car while making his rounds. He was a short, stout man with a thick Irish accent, not surprising since Ireland was the country of his birth. During the winter season, when business was slack, Barnes made an annual pilgrimage to his native land. When Barnes retired, he moved to Niagara-on-the-Lake where he lived for many more years. He is best remembered for a golfing trophy that bears his name. The Taylor Barnes Trophy is annually competed for at the last meeting of the season of the Western Ontario Greenkeepers Association.

Bill Aimers, a graduate from Guelph was superintendent for only one year at the Rosedale GC. Then he caught the bug to make money and that he did. His first enterprise was to operate a supply business to the golf course industry. Aimers sold ball washers, pins, flags, fertilizer, and pesticides. He was the first to call on golf courses in a panel truck loaded with his merchandise. One of his salesman was Bill McCracken who later branched out on his own and was succeeded by his son Dennis.

Bill Aimers's golf course business was thriving, but that was not good enough for this ambitious entrepreneur. He expanded into the homeowner market. First, he sold sprigs for lawns. Then he acquired a sod farm and supplied the booming residential housing market. Bill Aimers ran into some tough times for a while but he made a remarkable comeback with a wildflower business. The seeds of the wildflowers were sold in small packages and could be found in stores across the country.

Gerry Brouwer, a Dutch immigrant who grew sod in the flats near Lake Simcoe, invented a sod-harvesting machine that changed the industry. Brouwer manufactured the machine at a plant near Queensville, Ontario. He also made reel-bladed mowers and other machinery. This inventive genius was recognized beyond our borders before he even became famous at home.

Ron Craig is a relative latecomer to the golf industry scene. He started as a greensman with Don Burd at the Kleinburg GC, followed by a period at Oakdale GC with Bob Moote. Ron Craig graduated from the University of Guelph with a degree in horticulture. He soon realized that he had a future in selling machinery rather than growing grass. He started by selling "red" equipment for F. Manley, the Toro distributor. He switched to "orange" with Spramotor and then went back to "red" as a partner in Turf Care Products. He has expanded rapidly and acquired a full line of items from golf carts to fertilizer and leasing. With the aid of his thriving business, Ron Craig has been a reliable source of support for all superintendent activities. He served willingly on many different committees and for a while was president of the Ontario Turfgrass Research Foundation.

Ron Craig is still a young man with many years ahead of him, but he has already had an impact on our industry and we can only hope that his support will continue.

## *The Greatest Character of All*

Undoubtedly the most unique character in the turfgrass industry in Ontario has been Clinton Duke. Clinton Duke founded Duke Lawn Equipment Ltd. in Burlington, Ontario.

He made the name of his company famous in this province and beyond by annually organizing "Duke's Lawnorama." This big event drew participation not only from golf courses, but also from parks and municipal and government agencies. The Lawnorama not only featured equipment demonstrations but also music, celebrities, dancing girls, and often a barbershop quartet and a parade. At first the event was held at company headquarters on Plains Road, but the popularity of the occasion quickly made the move to more spacious quarters a necessity.

The ideal place was Duke's estate on Lake Ontario where Clinton and Bonnie Duke resided. It was called the Duke Research Centre because Clinton and his staff experimented and tested various mowers. The Research Centre was much more spacious and the annual Lawnorama continued to grow. Longtime visitors and friends were occasionally invited to Duke's private bomb shelter, which was well stocked for emergencies. Occasionally, Clinton would even demonstrate his machine gun, mounted on the back of a golf cart, by firing rounds into Lake Ontario. No harm was ever done but the cops got wind of it and Clinton had to pull in his horns. That little episode did not harm his thriving business, which has continued to grow and is now prospering under the direction of the third generation.

# Conclusion

In contemporary times, the modern golf course superintendent has achieved recognition and respect beyond the wildest dreams of the earliest practitioners of the art of greenkeeping. Yet, it was the early efforts of our forbears from over 100 years ago who made it all possible. These early pioneers recognized the need for education, cooperation with the colleges, and above all, the need to develop an association where like-minded individuals could exchange information and compare notes. Many may be forgotten, but some we have remembered in these pages. We must thank them all for what they accomplished in the beginning and hope that the current generation will learn from history and carry the torch into the future.

# Greenkeepers of
# the Twentieth Century

Every effort has been made to ensure that the following biographical information is as up-to-date and accurate as possible. This information has been compiled from the results of a survey submitted to all Ontario Golf Superintendents' Association members as well as from other longstanding members. We regret any omissions or errors that may occur in this listing.

| | | |
|---|---|---|
| Abbott, Jack | Islington GC | 1924–1938 |
| | Rosedale GC | 1939–1950 |
| | OGSA President | 1950–1962 |
| | GCSAA Director | |
| | | |
| Ablett, Courtney | Glen Cedars GC | 1973 |
| | | |
| Ackermann, Robert | Markland Woods, Supt. | 1992–present |
| | University of Guelph, B. Sc. Agr | 1989 |
| | | |
| Acton, Neil | Deer Creek G&CC | 1989–present |
| MS | Brooklea GC | 1980–1988 |
| | Niagara College Diploma | 1973–1979 |
| | University of Guelph Short Course | |
| | Co–founder of Georgian Bay Assn. | 1981 |
| | OGSA President | 1989 |
| | | |
| Alexander, Jeff | Parry Sound G&CC | 1996–present |
| | Seneca College Diploma | 1989 |
| | Cornell Short Course | 1993 |
| | Ohio State Short Course | 1998 |
| | | |
| Aljoe, Greg | Deer Ridge GC | present |
| | Foxwood GC | |
| | | |
| Allen, Ernie | Toronto Hunt Club | 1969 |
| | | |
| Allen, Gary | Westminster Trails, London | present |

| | | |
|---|---|---|
| Allen, Jeff | Rocky Crest Golf Resort | present |
| Allen, Ron | Donalda CC | 1973–1991 |
| Amos–Stock, Natalie | Harbour View G&CC | present |
| Amsler, Ernie | Angus Glen GC | 1992–present |
| | Manderin GC | |
| Anderson, John | IBM GC | |
| Anderson, Lamont | Point West GC | 1994–present |
| Arends, John | Centennial Park Golf Centre | 1987–1997 |
| | Hawthorn Valley GC | 1961–1987 |
| | University of Guelph Short Course | 1970 |
| | OGSA President | 1971 |
| Artis, George | Wildwood On The Lake G&CC | 1973 |
| Altoft, Chris | Picton G&CC | 1994–present |
| Arthur, Robert | Talbot GC | 1994–present |
| | Donalda GC | |
| Ashley, Charles | Norfolk G&CC | present |
| Austin, John | OGSA President | 1942–1947 |
| Baker, Dean | North Halton GC | 2001–present |
| | Glen Abby GC | 1989–present |
| Baker, Paul J. | Glen Cedars GC | 1973 |
| Baker, Robert | Seven Lakes GC | present |
| Barbeau, Capt. A.E. | CFB Rockcliffe | 1973 |
| Barnes, Paul | St. Clair Parkway GC | 1984–present |
| | Lambton College Parks Diploma | 1978 |
| | University of Guelph Short Course | 1985 |

| | | |
|---|---|---|
| Barnet, Kelly | Fox Glen GC | 1999–present |
| Barnett, Peter | Richmond Hill GC | 1994–present |
| Bartlett, Keith<br>MS | Thornhill CC<br>University of Guelph, B.Sc. Agr<br>OGSA president | 1992–present<br>1989<br>2000 |
| Baxter, Tim | Hickory Ridge G&CC | present |
| Beauchamp, Ryan | St. Thomas G&CC<br>Westminster Trails GC<br>University of Guelph Short Course | 1991–present<br>1990 |
| Bedour, Leroy | Goderich Sunset GC | present |
| Behm, Charles | Cherry Hill GC | 1969–1973 |
| Beeney, Alan | North Halton G&CC<br>University of Guelph Diploma<br>University of Guelph Short Course<br>OGSA President<br>Co–founder of OTRF | 1967–2000<br><br>1970<br>1977 |
| Bennett, Carl | Oakville Golf Club | 1973 |
| Bennett, John | London Hunt GC<br>Cedar Brae Golf Club | 1991<br>1973 |
| Bennett, Kevin | Westminster Trails GC | 1994 |
| Bishop, Ted | Rolling Meadows G&CC | 1994 |
| Blake, Joseph | Toronto Ladies GC<br>Fairvilla GC London | 1955<br>1966 |
| Bladon, John | Port Carling GC<br>Guelph Ladies G&CC | <br>1998–present |
| Bluett, L.C. | Mississaugua GC<br>CGSA President<br>OGSA President | 1969<br>1961–1962<br>1961–1962 |

| | | |
|---|---|---|
| Bontje, John | Circle Pine GC | 1994 |
| | Shelburne GC | present |
| | | |
| Booker, Randy | Dundas Valley G&CC | present |
| | Sleepy Hollow GC | 2000 |
| | | |
| Bond, Wm. | Essex GC | 1969 |
| | | |
| Bortolon, Aldo | Lookout Point GC | 1987–present |
| | University of Guelph Diploma | 1986 |
| | University of Guelph Short Course | 1980 |
| | | |
| Bouwhuis, Ted | Brockville CC | 1973 |
| | | |
| Bowen, Ian | Oshawa GC | 1992–present |
| | Lakeview GC | 1989–1991 |
| | University of Guelph Diploma | 1985 |
| | OGSA President | 1998–1999 |
| | | |
| Bowen, Wm | Dalewood GC | 1994–1996 |
| | Peterborough GC | 1969–1993 |
| | | |
| Bowers, Lennox | Hawkesbury G & Curling Club | 1973 |
| | | |
| Brackenbury, Jack | Kapuskasing GC | 1973 |
| | | |
| Bradley, Ernest | North Ridge GC, Brantford | 1969–1973 |
| | | |
| Brewster, Bob | Weston GC | 1970–1986 |
| | Toronto GC | 1987–1998 |
| | Mississaugua GC | 1999–present |
| | OGSA President | 1982 |
| | | |
| Breen, Doug | Conestoga GC | 2001 |
| | Calerin GC | 2000 |
| | | |
| Britton, Barry | Lionhead G&CC | |
| | Tyandaga Municipal GC | |

| | | |
|---|---|---|
| Brooke, David | Bradford Highland GC | 1996 |
| | DB Golf Course Consultants | present |
| | | |
| Brooks, Marc | Stone Tree GC | 1998–present |
| | Sawmill Creek G&CC | 1997 |
| | Bear Creek G&CC | 1988–1996 |
| | New Liskeard G&CC | 1987 |
| | Seneca Diploma | 1985 |
| | University of Guelph Diploma | 1986–1988 |
| | | |
| Brown, Paul G. | Sarnia Golf & Curling Club | 1997–present |
| | Maple Downs GC | 1988–1997 |
| | | |
| Brown, Paul R. | Islington GC | 1999–present |
| | | |
| Brown, Phil | Summit G&CC | 1996–present |
| | Forest City National GC | 1992–1995 |
| | Penn State Diploma | 1986–1988 |
| | | |
| Burger, Bruce | Lakeview GC | 1994–present |
| | Galt GC | |
| | Dalewood GC | |
| | OGSA President | 1994 |
| | | |
| Burgess, Jeff, | Weston GC | 1995–present |
| | CGCS, MS | |
| | | |
| Burns, John H. | Metro Parks Golf Courses | 1973 |
| | | |
| Burrows, Bob | Rosedale GC | 1997–present |
| | Hillsdale G&CC | 1993–1997 |
| | Cornwall G&CC | 1991–1993 |
| | U. of Massachusetts Diploma | 1990 |
| | University of Guelph Short Course | 1987 |
| | York University, B.A. Political Science 1982 | |
| | | |
| Burton, Mike | Heron Point Golf Links | present |
| | | |
| Butler, George | Scarborough GC | 1930 |

| | | |
|---|---|---|
| Butler, Richard | St. Andrew's East GC | 1994–present |
| Buttenham, Rick | Cranberry Resort | 1997–present |
| | Golfland | 1985–1988 |
| | University of Guelph Diploma | 1993 |
| | Cornell Short Course | 1995 |
| Cairncross, Cameron | Summit GC | 1973 |
| Caldwell, Dave | Carrying Place G&CC | present |
| Calhoun, Wm | Glen Eagle GC, Bolton | 1969–1973 |
| Campbell, Don | Blue Mountain G&CC | present |
| Carter, Jerry | Little River GC | 1973 |
| Carver, Brian | International CC | present |
| Chappell, Lloyd | Wingham G&CC | 1973 |
| Charlie, Terry | Cranberry Village GC | |
| | Old Castle GC | |
| Charman, Edward J. | London Hunt Club | 1973 |
| Charman, Fred | Toronto GC | 1973 |
| Charman, Jeff | Bolton GC | present |
| Charters, Thom | Bayview CC | 1995–present |
| | Weston G&CC | 1987–1995 |
| | Islington GC | 1977–1987 |
| | Penn State Diploma | 1976 |
| | OGSA President | 1988 |
| | Superintendent of the Year | 1992 |
| Cherry, David | Cherry Downs GC | |
| Cherry, John | National GC | 1994–1998 |
| | Cherry Downs GC | |

| | | |
|---|---|---|
| Chinery, Wm | York Downs GC | 1930 |
| Clapperton, Trevor | Dalewood G & Curling Club | present |
| Clark, Bruce | The Briars GC | 1994–1995 |
| | Emerald Hills GC | 1990–1993 |
| | Newmarket | 1988–1989 |
| | Midland G&CC | 1986–1988 |
| Clark, Edward | Pineland Greens GC | present |
| Clark, George | Board of Trade CC | 1973 |
| Clarridge, Tim | Parkview GC | present |
| Coderre, Marcel | Glen Shield Golf Club | 1973 |
| Coholan, Chris | Midland G&CC | present |
| Cole, Louis | Burlington GC | 1969–1973 |
| Colin, Tim | Carruther's Creek Golf Centre | present |
| Condon, John | Llyndonshire G&CC | present |
| Cooper, Alban | Rideau Glen GC | 1973 |
| Corbin, Robert N. | Cataraqui G&CC | 1973 |
| Cornfield, H.G. | Talisman Resort Hotel | 1973 |
| Cornish, Geoffrey | St. Charles GC | 1940 |
| Cote, Mike | Jewel of the North Golf Resort | present |
| | Glendale GC | |
| | Buttonville GC | |
| Courneya, Michael | Trillium Wood GC | present |

| | | |
|---|---|---|
| Cours, Dave | Erie Shores G&CC | 1990–present |
| | Marlwood G&CC | 1989–1990 |
| | St. Clair College Diploma | |
| | University of Guelph Short Course | |
| Cowan, Robert | Royal Woodbine GC | 1998–present |
| Corbin, Robert | Cataraqui GC Kingston | 1969 |
| Creed, Herbert | Westmount GC | 1969 |
| Creed, Michael | Wyldewood GC | 1994 |
| Creed, Richard | Cutten Club | present |
| Creighton, Peter | Toronto Hunt Club | 1994 |
| Cresswell, Robert | Pleasant Valley GC | present |
| Crissinger, Homer | Royal Ottawa GC | 1969 |
| Crymble, Don | Markham Green GC (prev. IBM) | 1993–present |
| | IBM CC | 1989–1992 |
| | Sleepy Hollow GC | 1981–1989 |
| | University of Guelph Assoc. | |
| | Diploma Agriculture | 1980 |
| Cunningham, John | Manderin G&CC | 1991–present |
| | Meadowbrook GC | 1979–1991 |
| | University of Guelph Diploma | |
| Currie, Todd | WestHaven G&CC | present |
| Cylka, Richard | Little River GC | 1973 |
| Daigle, Leo | Caledon GC | 1994 |
| Dale, A. S. | Kingsway Park GC | 1973 |
| DaMerino, Ernest C. | Root River GC | 1973 |

| | | |
|---|---|---|
| Darou, George | London Hunt Club | 1958 |
| | Richmond Hill GC | 1969–1973 |
| | OGSA President | 1965 |
| | | |
| Davidson, Douglas | Greystone GC | present |
| | | |
| Davy, Mark | Glendale G&CC | present |
| | | |
| Dawkins, Mark | Georgetown GC | present |
| | | |
| Dean, Robert Edward | Cornwall G&CC | 1973 |
| | | |
| DeCook, Jeff | Indian Creek GC | present |
| | | |
| Decorso, David | Victoria Park GC East | present |
| | | |
| Dermott, Paul | Oakdale G&CC | 1977–present |
| CGCS | Islington G&CC | 1972–1977 |
| | Chinguacousy CC | 1967–1972 |
| | University of Guelph Diploma | 1965 |
| | Penn State Diploma | 1967 |
| | OGSA President | 1975–1976 |
| | Superintendent of the Year Award | 1993 |
| | Founding Chairman of OTS | |
| | Founding Member of OTRF | |
| | Founding Member of Stanley Thompson Society | |
| | | |
| Dermott, Vince | Scenic Woods G&CC | present |
| | Markland Woods GC | 1991 |
| | | |
| Desilva, Sean | The Diamond "in the Ruff" GC | present |
| | | |
| Dew, Chris | Royal Woodbine GC | 1989–1997 |
| | National GC of Canada | 1998–present |
| | | |
| Dick, Dave | Scotts Company | 1977–present |
| | Sleepy Hollow G&CC | 1973–1977 |
| | University of Guelph Turf Short Course | 1974 |
| | University of Toronto, B Sc. | 1972 |

| Dickey, Peter | Glenway G&CC | 1989–present |
| | Streetsville Glen GC | 1988–1989 |
| | University of Guelph (ODH) | 1998–2000 |
| | Humber College Diploma | 1979–1980 |
| | | |
| Diggins, William | Country Lane GC | present |
| | | |
| Dimitriw, James | Lowville GC | present |
| | | |
| DiPinto, Sam | Lido Golf Centre | 1969 |
| | Beverly GC | |
| | | |
| Dixon, Robert | Pine Crest GC Ltd. | present |
| | | |
| Dlugokecki, Ray | Springfield G&CC | 1989–present |
| | University of Guelph | |
| | | |
| Doda, Ed | Barrie CC | present |
| | | |
| Dodson, Arthur | Maple Downs GC | 1960–1987 |
| | Summit GC | 1952–1959 |
| | OGSA President | 1964 |
| | McClumpha Tournament Chairman | 1953–1999 |
| | | |
| Dodson, Bruce | Hawkridge G&CC | 1989–1998 |
| | Emerald Hills G&CC | 1987–1989 |
| | Don Valley GC | 1984–1987 |
| | Dentonia Dr. GC | 1977–1984 |
| | Tam O'Shanter GC | 1971–1973 |
| | University of Guelph Diploma | 1974 |
| | | |
| Dodson, Paul | Silver Springs G&CC | 1998–present |
| | Lionhead G&CC | 1995–1998 |
| | Aurora Highlands G&CC | 1981–1995 |
| | Mississaugua G&CC | 1973–1980 |
| | Penn State Diploma | 1968 |
| | | |
| Dodson, Scott CGCS | Park CC of Buffalo | 1995–present |
| | Summit CC | 1995 |

| | | |
|---|---|---|
| Doering, Todd | Doon Valley/Rockway GC | present |
| Dolensky, Alex | Huntsville Downs G&CC | present |
| Donahue, Mike | City of Toronto Parks | 1973 |
| | Don Valley GC | 1969 |
| Dowling, Jason | Duntroon Highlands G&CC | present |
| | Woodington Lake GC | present |
| Draeken, Jakob | Strathroy CC | 1973 |
| Draper, Al | Greenhills GC | 1981 |
| | OGSA President | 1984 |
| Ducharme, Maurice | Mount Hope GC | 1969–1973 |
| | Pres. WOGSA | |
| Dunham, James | Sarnia G & Curling Club | 1973 |
| Dunn, Frank | Borden GC | 1969 |
| Dyker, Scott | Beverly GC | 1995–present |
| Dulong, Cory | Maitland GC | present |
| Dzvirka, George | Orchardview GC | present |
| Eberle, Charles | Ridgetown G&CC | 1975–present |
| | University of Guelph, B.Sc. Ag. | |
| Elliot, Sam | Royal Montreal GC | 1969 |
| Ellis, Ted | Blue Springs GC | present |
| CGCS | | |
| Engel, John | Ingersoll G&CC | 1973 |

| | | |
|---|---|---|
| Endicott, Barry | Nobleton Lakes G&CC | 1988–present |
| | Millcroft G&CC | 1986–1987 |
| | Chinguacousy G&CC | 1978–1986 |
| | Glen Shield G&CC | 1976–1977 |
| | OGSA President | 1986 |
| Endicott, Meryle (Curly) | Richbrook GC, Angus | 1969 |
| Erb, David | Garrison G & Curling Club | present |
| Evans, Craig CGSC | Pheasant Run GC | present |
| Evelyn, Sean | Ceder Hurst GC | 1999–present |
| | Streetsville Glen GC | 1996–1999 |
| | University of Guelph Short Course | 1979 |
| Fach, Bill MS CGCS | York Downs | 1997–present |
| | Rosedale GC | 1987–1997 |
| | Essex G&CC | 1977–1987 |
| | University of Waterloo | |
| | University of Guelph | |
| Faflak, George | Blenheim GC | 1973 |
| Fairbarn, Bruce | Sharon G&CC | 1973 |
| Farnsworth, Ed | Deerhurst Resort | present |
| Firth, James | Lakeview GC | 1965 |
| Findlay, Morley | Brantford GC | |
| | Maple City GC, Chatham | |
| | London Hunt GC | 1969–1973 |
| Finer, Mark | Lyderbrook GC | present |

| | | |
|---|---|---|
| Flett, Jim | Muskoka Lakes G&CC | 1992–present |
| | Blue Mountain G&CC | 1989–1991 |
| | Texas A&M Degree | 1984 |
| | University of Guelph Diploma | 1985 |
| Forrest, George | Pine Lake GC | present |
| Forrester, Wm | Weston GC | |
| Formosa, Louis | Lakeview GC | 1969 |
| Fortier, Rick | Lakewood GC | present |
| Francis, Doug | Little River GC | present |
| Fraser, Scott | CFB Trenton GC | present |
| French, Roy | Sturgeon Point GC | 1999–present |
| | Metropolitan Toronto Courses | |
| | Beverley G&CC | 1973 |
| | Lookout Pointe GC | 1969 |
| Froese, Richard | Oxley Beach GC | |
| Frost, Mac | Parkview GC | 1969 |
| | Brookwood GC | 1973 |
| | Spring Lakes GC | 1999 |
| Gall, John | Sault Ste. Marie GC | 1980–85 |
| | Oshawa GC | 1986–90 |
| | St. George's GC | 1990–present |
| Gardner, Scott | University of Guelph Diploma | 1992 |
| | Fanshawe Diploma | 1989 |
| | Greenhills G&CC | 1988–1990 |
| | Echo Valley GC | 1990–1994 |
| | Westhaven G&CC | 1994–1995 |
| | EchoValley GC | 1995–present |
| Garner, George | Glendale GC | |

| | | |
|---|---|---|
| Gatto, Rob | King Forest GC (City of Hamilton) | 1984–present |
| | Turf Management: | |
| | Ohio, Cornell, Guelph | 1995, 1994 |
| | | & 1992 |
| | | |
| George, Simon | Oakville GC | 1988–present |
| | Indian Wells GC | 1976–1988 |
| | University of Guelph Short Course | |
| | OGSA President | 1997 |
| | | |
| Giardine, J. R. | Spruce Needles GC | 1973 |
| | | |
| Gieseler, Marlon | Brooklea G&CC | present |
| | | |
| Gilmour, Troy | Lindsay G&CC | present |
| | | |
| Goodman, Chris | National Pines GC | present |
| | Cardinal GC | |
| | | |
| Gourlay, David S. | Summerlea GC, Montreal | 1992–1993 |
| | Thornhill GC | 1963–1992 |
| | Summit G&CC | 1960–1963 |
| | Pine Valley GC | 1957–1960 |
| | Kapuskasing GC | 1950–1957 |
| | Chedoke GC | 1948–1950 |
| | University of Guelph Short Course | 1970 |
| | University of Massachusetts | |
| |    Short Course | 1951 |
| | OGSA President | 1968 |
| | CGAA Distinguished Service Award | 1997 |
| | CGSAA Distinguished Service Award | 1987 |
| | Superintendent Award of the Year | |
| |    Score Award | 1982 |
| | | |
| Gourlay, David W. | Summerlea GC | 1994–1999 |
| | Colbert Hills GC | 1999–present |
| | Eagle Creek GC | 1990–1994 |
| | Ladies Club of Toronto | 1986 |
| | Beacon Hall GC | 1986–1989 |
| | OGSA President | 1993 |

| | | |
|---|---|---|
| Gravett, Gary | Saugeen GC | 1985–present |
| | University of Guelph Short Course | |
| | | |
| Gravett, John | Credit Valley GC | 1996–1998 |
| | Granite Club | 1999–present |
| | | |
| Gray, John | Essex GC | |
| | Border Cities GCSA Pres. | 1937 |
| | GCSAA Pres. | 1940 |
| | | |
| Grightmire, Fred | Dundas Valley GC | 1931 |
| | | |
| Grightmire, John | Rosedale GC | 1970–1987 |
| | Beverly G&CC | 1961–1970 |
| | Dundas Valley GC | 1945–1961 |
| | OGSA President | 1970 |
| | | |
| Grikinis, Raymond P. | Royal Lynn G&CC | 1973 |
| | | |
| Grosicki, Gary | Guelph CC | present |
| | Lakewood GC | |
| | Beachgrove CC | 1979–1983 |
| | | |
| Guertin, Henri | Chinguacousy CC | 1973 |
| | Bay of Quinte GC | 1969 |
| | | |
| Guthro, Frances | Black Creek GC | present |
| | | |
| Gutteridge, Michael | Ash Brook GC | present |
| | | |
| Guy, Charles | Highland GC | 1973 |
| | | |
| Hagen, Mark | Hyde Park Equipment | present |
| | West Haven G&CC | 1990 |
| | Wyldewood GC | |
| | OGSA President | 1991 |
| | | |
| Haines, Ross | Brampton GC | 1969–1973 |
| | | |
| Hall, Gary | Six Foot Bay GC | present |

| | | |
|---|---|---|
| Hall, Leslie | Six Foot Bay Resort & GC | 1955–present |
| | Ryerson Polytechnical Institute | 1966 |
| Hall, Robert | Georgetown GC | 1969–1973 |
| | Toronto Ladies GC | |
| Hallard, Steve | Cedar Brae G&CC | 1994–present |
| Hamilton, Thomas G. | Horseshoe Valley Resort | 1973 |
| Hannaford, Harold | Carleton GC | 1969–1973 |
| Harris, James | Knollwood GC | present |
| Harris, John | Elgin House , Muskoka | |
| | Uplands GC | |
| | St. Georges GC | |
| | Ancaster GC | |
| | Hamilton G&CC | |
| | Knollwood GC (owner) | 1970 |
| Harwood, Bob | Deer Run GC | present |
| Hastings, Gary | City of Kitchener Rockway | |
| | Doon Valley GC | present |
| Haus, Brian | Wooden Sticks GC | 1999–present |
| | Emerald Hills | |
| Hawkins, Fred | Lakeview GC | 1933 |
| | OGSA President | 1934–1941 |
| Hebert, Patrick | Roseland G & Curling Club | present |
| Heeson, Ron | Monterra G (Blue Mountain) | 1988–present |
| | Beach Grove G&CC | 1983–1988 |
| | University of Guelph Diploma | |
| Hempstead, Fred | Doon Valley GC | 1969–1973 |

| | | |
|---|---|---|
| Henderson, Ed | Beach Grove CC | 1973 |
| | Oakville GC | 1969 |
| | | |
| Heron, Robert | Beacon Hall GC | 1989–present |
| CGCS, MS | Mississaugua G&CC | 1981–1989 |
| | Markland Wood GC | 1969–1981 |
| | Brampton GC | 1968–1969 |
| | Penn State | 1964–1967 |
| | OGSAPresident | 1974 |
| | Score Superintendent of the Year | 1998 |
| | CGSA President | 1979 |
| | | |
| Heron, Scott | Bigwin Island GC | present |
| | | |
| Hickman, Jim | London Highland GC | 1920–1958 |
| | | |
| Hiles, Scott | Fredricton G & Curling Club | present |
| | | |
| Hoekstra, Cecil | Cherry Hills GC | present |
| | | |
| Holmes, D. F. | Derrydale GC | 1973 |
| | | |
| Holmes, Steve | Maple Downs G&CC | 1998–present |
| | | |
| Homewood, Richard | OGSA President | 1948–1949 |
| | | |
| Honeyball, Jason | King Valley GC | 1999–present |
| | | |
| Hooper, Randall | Beach Grove G&CC | present |
| CGCS | Sawgrass | |
| | Roseland GC | |
| | | |
| Hopkins, James | Fawn Brook GC | present |
| | | |
| Howald, Caleb | Woodington Lake | present |
| | Hockley Valley Resort | |
| | | |
| Hughes, John | Horseshoe Valley Resort | present |
| | | |
| Humble, Michael | Savannah Golf Links | present |

| | | |
|---|---|---|
| Hutchison, John | Warkworth GC | 1973–present |
| Hynds, Wm | St. Georges GC<br>OGSA President<br>Score Superintendent of the year | 1969–1989<br>1972 |
| Ireland, Jason | Owen Sound GC | 1969–1973 |
| Ireton, John | Conestoga GC | present |
| Jenkins, Clarence | Cataraqui G&CC<br>Trenton CC | present<br>1973 |
| Jenkins, Shorty | World Famous Ice Maker<br>Bay of Quinte GC<br>Cataraqui GC | present<br><br>2000 |
| Janzen, Cory | Toronto Board of Trade CC | 1999–present |
| Jones, Allen | Aurora Highlands GC<br>OGSA President | 1955–1980<br>1969 |
| Johnson, Donald | Indian Hills GC | 1973 |
| Johnson, Ken | Indian Hills GC | present |
| Johnston, Tom | Carling Lake GC | 1969 |
| Jones, Eric | Niagara–on–the–Lake GC | 1973 |
| Jones, Stephen | Oakville Exec GC | present |
| Kaleta, Henry | Bowmanville G&CC | present |
| Kaster, Weston | Dundee GC | 1973 |
| Keffer, Andrew | Rattlesnake Point GC | present |
| Keith, David | Burlington Springs GC | 1973 |

| | | |
|---|---|---|
| Kellog, Gavin | Tyandaga Municipal GC | present |
| Kennedy, Robert | Garden City Municipal GC | 1981 |
| | OGSA President | 1987 |
| Kinch, Peter | Emerald Hills GC | present |
| Kirkpatrick, Hugh | Westmount G&CC | 1978–present |
| | Dalewood GC | 1973–1978 |
| | Conestoga GC | 1968–73 |
| | C.E. Robinson & Associates | 1963–1968 |
| | OGSA President | 1985 |
| | Superintendent of the Year | 1997 |
| Klassen, Jacob J. | Merry–Hill GC Ltd. | 1973 |
| Klingenberg, Mans | Craigowan G&CC | 1973 |
| Konarowski, John | Kedron Dells | 1970–present |
| | Grandview GC | 1973 |
| | University of Guelph Short Course | |
| Kopp, Helmut | St. Georges GC | 1989 |
| | St. Charles GC | 1977–1987 |
| | Essex GC | 1975–1977 |
| | Uplands GC | 1969–1973 |
| Kopp, Martin | Lionhead G&CC | 1998–present |
| | Kleinburg GC | |
| Kulak, Jay | Port Colourne CC | present |
| Kulak, Jon | Dunnville G&CC | present |
| Kulba, Don | Maple of Ballantrae | 2000 |

| | | |
|---|---|---|
| LaBelle, Alex | Paris G&CC | 1999–present |
| CGSA,MS | Highlands Links GC | 1998 |
| | Merry–Hill GC | 1994–1998 |
| | Carleton G & Yacht Club | 1986–1994 |
| | Midland G&CC | !982–1986 |
| | Bordon Circle Pine GC | 1981 |
| | University of Guelph Short Course | |
| | Biology Degree | |
| | OGSA President | 1996 |
| | | |
| Ladouceur, Frank | Idylwylde GC | 1973–1996 |
| | Rivermeade GC | 1973 |
| | | |
| Ladouceur, Normand | Glen Sheilds GC | 1969 |
| | Rivermead GC | |
| | | |
| Laferriere, Gerry | Cedar Green G&CC | present |
| | | |
| Lamanna, Rocco | Bloomington Downs GC | present |
| | | |
| Lamb, Robert | Summit G & CC | 1973 |
| | | |
| Lavis, Dan | Ingersoll G&CC | present |
| | | |
| Lagato, Ron | Scenic Woods GC | present |
| | | |
| Lelievre, Derek | Derrydale GC | 1997–present |
| | Greenhills CC | 1991–1994 |
| | Greenwood GC | 1988–1990 |
| | Huron Oaks CC | 1987 |
| | University of Guelph Degree | 1995, 1991 |
| | | |
| Lemieux, Paul | Kingsville G&CC | present |
| | | |
| Lewis, W.G. (Tommy) | Kawartha GC | 1969–1973 |
| | Retired after 55 years as | |
| | Superintendent | |
| | | |
| Louth, George | Twenty Valley GC | 1973 |

| | | |
|---|---|---|
| Lucas, Peter | Bay of Quinte GC | 1995–present |
| | Cedar Brae G&CC | 1994–1995 |
| Lynch, Gary | Woodland Links | present |
| Mackay, Allan | Ainsdale GC | present |
| Mackay, Donald | Muskoka Highlands GC | present |
| MacDonald, Bernard | Green Acres GC | 1969–1973 |
| MacDonald, Norman | Summit GC | present |
| | York Downs GC | |
| Macey, Jeff | Idylwylde G&CC | 1997–present |
| Magwood, Mike | Niagara–on–the–Lake GC | present |
| Malott, Mark | Belleview GC | present |
| Malott, Quin | Innerkip Highlands GC | present |
| Margetts, Tom | River Edge GC | present |
| Martin, Bernie | Hunters Glen GC | present |
| | Tyandaga    Municipal GC | |
| Martin, Tony | Trenton | present |
| Matthews, Reg | Beaverdale GC | 1973 |
| Maw, Arthur | Evergreen GC | present |
| McArthur, Elwood | Scarborough GC | 1956–1977 |
| McBean, Ian | St. Clair Parkway GC | 1973 |
| McCaffrey, Brent | Carrying Place GC | present |
| McClumpha, Alex | Elms GC | |
| | Thornhill CC | 1942–1963 |
| | OGSA President | 1953–1956 |
| | Founder: Alex McClumpha Tourn. | 1947 |

McClumpha, Bill    IBM GC

McClure, Mark      Burford Golf Links                          present

McFaul             Hamilton G&CC
                   Glenn Abbey GC                              1982–1987

McGee, Ross J.     Big Bay Point CC                            1973

McLeod, Alex       Turf Care Products                         1998–present
                   Spring Lakes GC                             1994–1998
                   Hockey Valley Resort

McMaster, Blake    Royal Montreal GC                          1995–present
                   Brampton GC                                 1975–1995
                   Carrying Place GC                           1974
                   Gormley Green GC                            1973
                   Toronto Ladies GC                           1970–1973
                   University of Guelph Short Course           1973
                   Guelph Advanced Turf Short Course           1976
                   Ryerson Business Diploma
                   Score Superintendent of the Year
                   CGSA President

McMullin, Norman   Sault Ste. Marie GC                         1969

McNeil, Allin J.   Base Borden G & Curling Club                1973

Mellon, Harry      St. Andrews GC                              1955

Meyer, Douglas     Cedarbrook GC                               present
                   CGCS, MS

Mickalko, Paul     Mad River GC                                present

Miller, Stephen    Dundas Valley GC                            1974
                   Burlington GC                               1994
                   UBC Degree
                   President CGSA                              1984

| | | |
|---|---|---|
| Miller, Jason | Golf Shape Development Inc. (Arch.)<br>U. of Guelph Degree (Geography) | 1991–present<br>1984 |
| Mills, Alan | South Muskoka G.and CC | present |
| Mills, Stuart | Essex GC<br>Hamilton GC<br>Highland CC<br>OGSA President | 1977–1986<br><br>1997<br>1979 |
| Milne, Ron | Harmony Creek GC (Supt)<br>Langside Diploma<br>University of Guelph Short Course | 1993–present |
| Mongeon, Herve | Club de Golf Outauais | 1969–1973 |
| Moore, James | Puslinch Lake GC<br>Science Hill GC (Const)<br>University of Guelph Short Course | 1980–present<br>1973–1979<br>1977 |
| Moote, Bob | R.F. Moote & Associates Ltd.<br>Oakdale G&CC<br>Stanley Thompson & Associates<br>University of Guelph Degree and<br>    Short Course<br>OGSA President | <br>1977<br><br><br><br>1967 |
| Moote, David | Rosedale GC<br>Essex GC<br>Scarboro GC<br>OGSA President<br>GCSAA President | 1969<br>1970–1977<br>1977<br>1959–1960<br>1964 |
| Mudie, John | Riverview GC | 1973 |
| Mulligan, Reg | King Valley GC<br>University of Guelph | 1997–1999<br>1991 |
| Mulroy, Dan | Kleinburg GC<br>Seneca Diploma | present |

| Murphy, Tom | Lambton G&CC | present |
| Murtagh, Carl | Kingsville G & Curling Club | 1973 |
| Muys, Steven | Twenty Valley GC | |
| Muylaert, Charles | Pine Valley GC | 1969–1973 |
| Muylaert, Rene | Chinguacousy GC<br>Muylaert & Associates GC<br>Architects | |
| Neff, Bill | Indian Creek GC (owner) | 1980–present |
| Nelson, Ken<br>CGCS | Sutton Creek GC<br>City of Regina Parks<br>Sunningdale GC<br>OSGA President | 1984<br><br>1981<br>1981 |
| Nimmo, Gord<br>CGCS | Holiday Inn GC<br>Sarnia GC<br>OGSA President | present<br><br>1990 |
| Nisbit, Colin | Westview GC<br>University of Guelph Diploma<br>U. of Mass. Short Course | 1985–present<br><br>1984 |
| Nisbet, Keith | Westview GC (owner/founder)<br>Aurora Highlands<br>OGSA President<br>GCSAA Board<br>Mayor, Town of Aurora<br>President Ontario Golf Association | 1957–present<br>12 years<br>1966<br>4 years |
| Norwood, Ernest | Chedoke Civic GC | 1973 |
| O'Connor, Dan | Greenwood GC | present |
| O'Donnell, Ed | Big Bay Pointe G&CC | present |

| | | |
|---|---|---|
| O'Donnell, Helen | Baldoon GC | present |
| O'Heron, Greg | Peterborough G&CC<br>Markland Woods CC | present |
| Oleniuk, George | Wawonash GC | 1973 |
| Olsen, N. | Strathcona GC | 1973 |
| Ortieb, Ed | Bayview GC<br>Doon Valley GC | 1969–1973 |
| Oswald, Art | Whitevale GC | present |
| Outred, Richard | Diamond Back G&CC | |
| Ouwendyk, Rob | Haggersville GC | present |
| Panasuik, Nick | Hydeway GC | present |
| Pandolfi, Rino | Uplands G & Ski Club | present |
| Parker, Jeff | Fort William CC | present |
| Parker, John | Trafalgar GC | present |
| Patterson, Kenneth | Centennial Park GC | present |
| Pattinson, Robert | London Hunt G&CC | present |
| Payne, George | Uplands GC | 1973 |
| Pellrene, Dennis | Capilano GC, Vancouver<br>Scarborough GC<br>Glen Abbey GC<br>Superintendent of the Year | present<br>1984–1994<br>1973–1984<br>2000 |
| Perrault, Richard | The Oaks G&CC | present |
| Piccolo, John | St. Catherines GC<br>Pres. WOGSA | 1973 |

| | | |
|---|---|---|
| Piccolo, Mark | Galt Country Club<br>Humber and University of<br>Guelph Diplomas | 1992–present |
| Piccolo, Rick | Brantford GC | 1992–present |
| Piccolo, Vince | Brantford GC | 1973 |
| Pickard, John | Maple City GC | present |
| Price, Art | Credit Valley GC | 1969 |
| Prozak, Doug | Blairhampton GC | present |
| Putney, Gordon | Sunset Golf Centre | 1973 |
| Rasmus, Keith | Scarborough GC | present |
| Rasmus, Kurt | Ballantrae GC | present |
| Rath, Wayne<br>CGCS | Islington GC<br>Magna International GC | 1988–1998<br>1999–present |
| Reeve, Ab | Whitevale GC | 1969–1973 |
| Reid, Joseph | Woodbridge GC<br>Elmira GC | |
| Reilly, Lloyd | Cutten Club, Guelph<br>Northwood CC, Downsview<br>Glendale GC<br>OGSA President | 1950<br>1958<br>1969–1973<br>1957–1958 |
| Rennie, Blair | Unionville Fairways Golf Centre<br>Diamondback GC | 1986–1994<br>1999–present |
| Rennie, Nigel | Unionville Fairways Golf Centre | 1982–1985 |
| Richard, Jerry | Oxford G&CC<br>University of Guelph Diploma | 1989–present<br>1985 |

| | | |
|---|---|---|
| Richards, Ray | Mad River GC<br>CFB Borden G&CC | present |
| Roberts, Jim | Sunningdale CC | 1973 |
| Roberts, Joe | Oshawa GC | 1973 |
| Robertson, Donald J. | Maplewood GC | 1973 |
| Robertson, William | Port Colborne CC | 1973 |
| Robinson, Robert | Hidden Lake GC | present |
| Romahn, Paul | Elmira GC<br>Dundee CC<br>University of Guelph Short Course/<br>Advanced<br>U of Mass. Short Course | 1987–present<br>1985–1986<br><br>1985, 1987<br>1986 |
| Salonen, Kimmo | Spring Lakes GC<br>Port Carling GC<br>Windemere Resort, Muskoka<br>York Downs GC | 1997–2000<br>1990<br>1991–1997<br>1971–1990 |
| Sansom, Wm | Toronto GC<br>OGSA President<br>GCSAA President | 1915–1935<br>1924–1934 |
| Sara, Jim | Streetsville Glen G&CC | |
| Scenna, Paul | Donalda Club<br>University of Guelph Diploma<br>Cornell Short Course | 1992–present<br>1989<br>1991 |
| Scenna, Pelino<br>MS | Burlington G&CC<br>Galt CC<br>Brantford G&CC<br>University of Guelph Short Course<br>OGSA President 1997<br>CGSA President | 1985–present<br>1963–1985<br>1957–1963<br><br><br>1978 |

| | | |
|---|---|---|
| Schaly, Tim | Briar Fox GC | 1998–present |
| | Dragon Fly Golf Links | 1997–1998 |
| | Golf Shape Development Inc. | 1996 |
| | Seneca Diploma | 1991 |
| Schaller, John B. | C.F.B. Trenton GC | 1973 |
| Schmelefske, Dave | Ontario Seed Co. | present |
| | Pine Lake GC | 1986–1996 |
| | Merry Hill GC | 1989–1994 |
| | OGSA Director | 1993 |
| Schneider, Mark | Owen Sound G&CC | 1993–present |
| | Beach Grove G&CC | 1988–1992 |
| | University of Guelph Diploma | |
| | and Short Course | 1985, 1983 |
| Schutz, Gerd | Pinewood Park GC | 1973 |
| Schwemler, Albert | Toronto GC | 1999–present |
| | York Downs GC | 1990–1995 |
| | University of Guelph, BSc (Agr) | 1987 |
| | University of Windsor, BSc (Geology) | 1984 |
| Scott, James | Bradford Highlands | |
| Scott, M. B. | Canard Valley G&CC | 1973 |
| Scott, Randy MS | Kanawaki GC | present |
| Sealey, Edward | Mahoning Valley GC | present |
| Sellers, Carl | Tam O'Shanter GC | 1969–1973 |
| Serrao, Rick | Glendale G&CC | |
| | Ingersol G&CC | |

| | | |
|---|---|---|
| Shantz, Allan | Dundas Valley GC | 1975–1999 |
| | Whirlpool GC | 1974 |
| | Niagara Parks Diploma | 1975 |
| | University of Guelph Short Course | |
| | & Advanced | 1976 |
| Shea, Wm. E. | Muskoka Lakes G&CC | 1973 |
| Sheilds, Hugh | Talbot Park GC | present |
| Shouldice, Graham | Highland GC | 1974–present |
| | London Hunt & CC | 1962–1972 |
| | University of Guelph Short Course | |
| | Phys. Ed. Degree | |
| Simpson, Tom | Newcastle GC (Supt/Owner) | 1965–present |
| Simms, Peter | Idylwylde G&CC | 1995–1997 |
| Sizer, Brad | Brier Fox GC | |
| Sloan, Robert | Cardinal GC | 1995–present |
| | Idylwyde GC | 1988–1995 |
| Smith, Blair | Bancroft GC | present |
| Smith, David | Muskoka Lakes G&CC | |
| Smith, Greg | Muskoka Highlands GC | present |
| Smith, John | Kawartha G&CC | present |
| | Wyldewood G&CC | 1973 |
| Somerville, Gordon | Oshawa GC | 1990–1993 |
| Speake, Rod | Deer Creek G&CC | present |
| St. Denis, Tom | Murry Hills GC | present |
| Stainton, Brent | Peel Village GC | present |

| | | |
|---|---|---|
| Stairs, Gary | Bushwood GC | present |
| Stanev, Jordan | Streetsville Glen GC | present |
| Stannard, Reg | IBM CC | 1969–1973 |
| Starostic, Phil | Dunnville G&CC | 1973 |
| Stauffer, Jeff | Credit Valley GC | 1999–present |
| | University of Guelph Diploma | 1993 |
| | Cornell Short Course | 1997 |
| Steel, John B. | St. Charles GC, Manitoba | 1944–1977 |
| | Canadian Golf Hall of Fame | |
| | GCSAA Distinguished Service Award | |
| | 1st CGSA president | 1966 |
| Stein, John | Ladies GC of Toronto | 1986–present |
| Stephenson, Keith | Haliburton Highland GC | |
| Stevens, David | Beaverbrook GC | present |
| Stevens, Robert | Crosswinds G&CC | present |
| Stirling, Gerald | Bluewater GC | 1973–present |
| Stormes, Peter | White Witch GC | |
| Stoughton, John | Barrie GC | 1969–1973 |
| Styles, Tom | St. Catherines GC | 1920 |
| Summers, Bruce | Pickering GC  50 years | 1973 |
| | Lakeridge GC | |
| | Winchester GC | |
| Suter, Douglas | Credit Valley GC | 1973–1995 |
| | Mono Hills GC | 1999 |

| | | |
|---|---|---|
| Sutherland, Gary | Osprey Valley GC | present |
| Sutherland, John | Hamilton GC | 1901–1937 |
| Svab, David | Victoria Park GC West | present |
| Szturm, Charles | Pine Knot GC | present |
| Tascone, David | Granite Ridge GC | present |
| Taylor, John | Hunters Pointe GC | present |
| | Twenty Valley GC | 1982–1999 |
| | Seneca Diploma | 1982 |
| | OGSA President | 1995 |
| Telfer, David M. | Garson Golf & CC | 1973 |
| Thompson, Nicol | Niagra Parks GC | 1969 |
| Thompson, Wm. | Islington GC | 1969 |
| Thompson, Jeremy | Sandhills Golf Resort | present |
| Thorton, Bill | Wildwood GC | present |
| Tom, Ted | Innisfil Creek GC | present |
| Toombs, Eugene | Southern Pines G&CC | 1973 |
| Trainor, Rhod | Hamilton G&CC | 1990–present |
| CGCS | St. Thomas G&CC | 1982–1990 |
| | Chippewa CC | 1979–1982 |
| | University of Guelph Diploma | 1976 |
| | OGSA President | 1992 |
| Uens, Art | Meadowbrook GC | 1969–1973 |
| Unsworth, Tom | Toronto Ladies GC | |
| | St. Thomas G&CC | 1973 |
| | OGSA President | 1963 |

| Unsworth, Wayne | Maple City CC | 1973 |
| | Grandview GC | 1969 |
| Uzelac, Dan | Dominion GC | 1969–1986 |
| Vandenburg, Henri | Dundas Valley GC | 1969–1973 |
| Van Veld, Art | Simord Golf Links | 1988–1998 |
| | Timber Ridge GC | 1999–present |
| Van Zanten, John | Kanata Golf & CC | 1973 |
| Vermette, Ronald, R. | Tilbury G & Curling Club | 1973 |
| Verrall, Stephen | Royal Ottawa GC | 1988–present |
| | Cataraqui GC | 1982–1988 |
| | University of Guelph Short Course | 1979 |
| Vollett, Bruce | Foxwood GC | present |
| Von Cube, Bernd | Cambridge G&CC | present |
| Vout, Warren | Brampton GC | present |
| | Cedar Brae GC | |
| Wallace, Wilfrid J. | Willo–Dell GC Inc. | 1973 |
| Walton, Daniel | Seaton GC | present |
| | Oshawa GC | 1985 |
| Warkman, Rusty | Stratford CC | 1973 |
| | OGSA President | 1983 |
| Warner, Mark | Lombard Glen G&CC | present |
| Weatherson, Alex | Glen Cedars GC | present |
| Webb, Tim | Sunningdale GC | present |
| Wheeler, Scott CGCS | Forest City National GC | present |

| | | |
|---|---|---|
| Whibley, James Ronald | Eldale Valley G&CC | 1973 |
| | | |
| White, Paul | The Briars G&CC | 1999–present |
| MS | Mississaugua G&CC | 1989–1998 |
| | Glen Abbey GC | 1988 |
| | Lambton G&CC | 1979–1987 |
| | Glendale G&CC | 1972–1978 |
| | Kanawaki GC | 1967–1971 |
| | U of Mass. Diploma | |
| | OGSA President | 1980 |
| | CGSA President | 1992 |
| | | |
| Wiechers, Dan | North Granite Ridge GC | present |
| | | |
| Wilder, Norman | Lakewood GC | 1973 |
| | | |
| Wilkinson, Dan | Woodlands Links Ltd | present |
| | | |
| Williams, Karl | Unionville Fairways Golf Centre | 1964–1981 |
| | | |
| Winters, Roseann | Frog's Breath GC | present |
| | | |
| Witteveen, Gordon | London Highland GC | 1958–1960 |
| MS | Northwood GC | 1961–1972 |
| | Board of Trade GC | 1973–1999 |
| | University of Guelph B.Sc. | 1958 |
| | CGSA President and founding | |
| | member | 1970 |
| | Superintendent of the Year | |
| | Leo Feser Award | |
| | J.B. Steel Award | |
| | Author: Practical Golf Course | |
| | Maintenance | 1998 |
| | A Century of Greenkeeping | 2001 |
| | | |
| Witteveen, Sid | Loch Marsh GC | 1985–present |
| | Vaughan Valley GC | 1981–1985 |
| | University of Guelph Short Course | |

| Woolley, Bruce | St. Georges GC | |
| | Markland Woods GC | |
| | City of Toronto GC | |
| | Won 1st McClumpha Tournament | 1947 |

| Wright, Ken | Devils Pulpit and Paintbrush | present |
| | Northwood GC | 1969 |
| | National GC | 1993 |

| Wyllie, David | Kings Riding/Aurora Highlands | 1998–present |
| | Evelyn Golf Centre | |
| | York Downs GC | |
| | Penn State University | 1994–1995 |

| Wyllie, James | James A. Wyllie Assc. (Pres.) | 1987–1997 |
| | Bayview CC | 1979–1994 |
| | Lambton G&CC | 1967–1979 |
| | Huntington GC | 1960–1967 |
| | Cutten Club | 1956–60 |
| | University of Guelph Short Course | 1971 |
| | OGSA President | 1973 |
| | CGSA President | 1975 |
| | GCSAA President | 1982 |
| | USGA Green Section Advisor | 1980–1986 |
| | Chairman Seneca College turf program | |

| Yates, Thomas | Castlemore G&CC | present |

| Zettler, Alan | Walkerton GC | present |

# About the Author

Gordon Witteveen was born in The Netherlands in 1934 and upon arrival in Canada some twenty years later, attended the Ontario Agricultural College in Guelph. During summer vacations he developed a love of golf while working at the Noranda Mines Golf Course in the province of Quebec. Upon graduation from college (1958), he became the superintendent at London Highland Country Club. After three years he moved to Toronto and for twelve years was the superintendent at the now defunct Northwood Golf Course. It was during this period that he became involved with the Ontario Golf Superintendent's Association and later helped start the Canadian Golf Superintendent's Association.

He initiated The *Green Master* magazine and served as its editor for five years. Witteveen also served on the Golf Course Superintendent's Association of America as a director and remains active in that association as a member of the Historical Preservation Committee.

In 1973 he became Superintendent of the 36-hole Board of Trade Country Club which he expanded to 45 holes by designing and constructing the 9-hole south course just a few years later. Since retiring from the Board of Trade in 1999, Witteveen reopened a dormant 9-hole layout near Brantford. The Pleasant View Golf Club is owned and operated by the Witteveen family.

Gordon Witteveen is a world traveler who has visited and played golf courses all over the globe. Often during his travels he made presentations such as "25 Years of Mistakes." Together with his colleague, Michael Bavier from Chicago, Witteveen co-authored a book titled *Practical Golf Course Maintenance*. A seminar based on the book *The Magic of Greenkeeping* has been presented all over Canada, the USA, and beyond. Witteveen is regular columnist for a number of magazines, and he has received the Leo Feser Award for writing excellence in the *American Golf Course Management* magazine. He is also a teacher and lecturer, but his most lasting contribution to golf is the many young men and women he has mentored who have followed in his footsteps.